The Environment: A Primary Teacher's Guide

Don Plimmer, Eric Parkinson and Kevin Carlton

CASSELL

Cassell
Wellington House
125 Strand
London WC2R 0BB

215 Park Avenue South
New York
NY 10003

British Library Cataloguing-in-Publication Data
A catalogue record for this book is available from the British Library.

ISBN 0-304-33353-0 (hardback)
    0-304-33355-7 (paperback)

Typeset by York House Typographic Ltd
Printed and bound in Great Britain by Redwood Books, Trowbridge, Wiltshire

THE ENVIRONMENT

WITHDRAWN

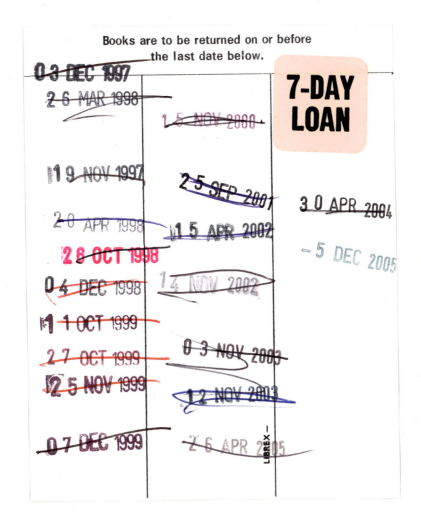

Books are to be returned on or before
the last date below.

0 3 DEC 1997

2 6 MAR 1998

1 5 NOV 2000

7-DAY LOAN

1 9 NOV 1997

2 5 SEP 2001

3 0 APR 2004

2 0 APR 1998

1 5 APR 2002

- 5 DEC 2005

2 6 OCT 1998

0 4 DEC 1998

1 4 NOV 2002

1 1 OCT 1999

2 7 OCT 1999

0 3 NOV 2003

2 5 NOV 1999

1 2 NOV 2003

0 7 DEC 1999

2 6 APR 2005

LIBREX —

Also available from Cassell:

K. Carlton and E. Parkinson: *Physical Sciences: A Primary Teacher's Guide*
T. Jarvis: *Children and Primary Science*
M. Watts: *Science in the National Curriculum*
P. Wiegand: *Children and Primary Geography*
M. Williams (ed.): *Understanding Geographical and Environmental Education*

Contents

Preface

Welcome to the second of the Primary Teacher's Guide series. This book on the environment expresses part of a natural progression from the first volume on Physical Sciences.

The word 'environment' seems to be on everybody's lips these days, yet how many of us really understand what the term means? To help make some sense of all this, we have chosen to present this book as an environmental science reader rather than just an 'environmentalist's' book. We are concerned that we take a scientific approach in order to avoid falling into the common traps of popular misconceptions about the world of which we are a part.

We begin in Chapter 1 by considering the Earth as a finite resource rather than an unbounded source of riches for us to enjoy without a wider sense of responsibility. We also take a look over our shoulder at our less than harmonious past.

Chapters 2 and 3 are concerned with humanity and its place within the whole scope of life on our Earth.

Chapters 4, 5, 6, 7 and 8 are focused on some of the ways in which our everyday actions impinge on our fellow travellers through space as we share our common planet. In these chapters, we wish to stress the importance of *we* in the context of our actions, rather than *they*, to emphasize the fact that we are all responsible for the consequences.

In Chapter 9 we look to the future and try to assess the impact of various outcomes of ways in which we currently live our lives.

Chapter 1

Spaceship Earth

Perhaps the famous view looking back at Earth from the first lunar exploration did much to make more people realize that 'spaceship Earth' was indeed a self-contained, finite resource.

Undoubtedly we all need to adopt more responsible attitudes to the environment, that is, to our home planet, Earth, and to the varied forms of life it sustains. It is in our primary schools that some of the foundations are laid for these attitudes.

Until quite recently the knowledge required to understand the environment was largely the domain of a quite small band of specialized scientists who studied the subject of 'ecology'. Knowledge of various ecological problems has become serious and widespread enough to attract the attention of the media. As a consequence, the terms 'ecology' and 'environment' have begun increasingly to enter the language of politicians and to become matters of concern to a wider range of people. Unfortunately, as is so often the case with science, the subject has been 'hijacked' by non-scientists who are more vocal than much of the scientific community but who lack any fundamental knowledge of the principles involved.

So what, then, do these terms 'environment' and 'ecology' really mean? Let us start with 'environment'. The Oxford English Dictionary defines the word environment as follows: 'The conditions or influences under which any person or thing lives'. This is not a bad start to our understanding for it demonstrates that the term embraces all the conditions affecting the life of living organisms. This, of course, includes ourselves, since humanity is not above the environment but exists within it and forms an integral part of it.

It is important to appreciate that this means both the **abiotic** environment, that is the physical conditions, such as light, water supply, chemicals, structure of surroundings, and so on, and also the **biotic** environment. This biotic environment consists of all the living things which occupy the same physical space and which may in some way impinge on each others' lives. When we think of living things we may initially only think of green plants and animals. However fungi, which are non-green plants, bacteria and viruses are all important components of our biotic environment, as anyone who has suffered from interaction with the last two will be only too well aware! It is often the effects of the physical environment – pollution, acid rain, and so on – which attract widespread concern, whereas the implications of changes to the biotic environment may be more far-reaching although often receiving less publicity.

Most people probably have some idea, albeit a restricted one, of what the term 'environment' means. The term 'ecology' is, however, frequently misused. Ecology is often spoken of as if it were a 'thing' whereas, in fact, it is a field of study. The word is derived from two Greek words, *oikos*, house or dwelling, and *logos*, discourse, and is concerned with the study of living things as they *really* are – not preserved in a bottle or pressed in a book!

Ecology deals not only with living things but also with the places in which they live and the way they react with their surroundings and with each other. The excitement of studying ecology is that it provides us with insights into some of the greatest problems and challenges facing us all, both locally and globally. Appreciation of our planet must be more than an aesthetic feeling of harmony with nature. It cannot simply be based on emotive issues such as the slaughter of baby seals for example. It must be based on an understanding of the fundamental principles of ecology which become as much part of our culture as the language we speak. Only then will we be able to react to questions of waste disposal, conservation of plant and animal species, and all aspects of pollution by using our heads as well as our hearts.

A major obstacle to managing the environment successfully is ignorance. One of the first problems we face is counteracting the very fundamental idea that the Earth is so large and its resources so vast that mankind can go on increasing in numbers, plundering natural resources, and putting our waste in 'empty' spaces without significantly altering the environment.

Policies on the environment will be made by governments but, unless these politicians are elected by a more knowledgeable electorate, it is likely that they will continue to make decisions which may, in the long term, have disastrous consequences. The Earth's environment simply cannot stand a continuation of mistakes such as those which have led to the partial destruction of the ozone layer or the steady pollution of the oceans. Because the future of our environment is so much influenced by the actions of us humans, much of this book will be concerned with these effects. However, in order to understand what are often very far-reaching effects we must first understand some fundamental principles of ecology, and this is where we shall start.

FIRST, HOWEVER, SOME TECHNICAL TERMS EXPLAINED …

One of the first, key ideas to appreciate about the environment is that one is always dealing with a system, not a series of unrelated events.

To clarify this important idea ecologists prefer to use more specific terms than just 'environment'. One of the most important of these is the term **ecosystem**. Ecosystems vary greatly in size and complexity and some have much more precise boundaries than others. For example, a pond is an ecosystem in which the boundaries are clearly defined whereas a grassland ecosystem may merge almost imperceptibly into an adjoining woodland ecosystem. In general, aquatic ecosystems will have more clearly defined boundaries but may vary greatly in size. Thus a pond may be a very small one whereas the open ocean is the largest ecosystem unit. The key idea of an ecosystem is that it is a more or less discrete system which is defined by both its physical conditions and the interactions of the creatures within it.

Although we can study an individual ecosystem as a unit no ecosystem is, in reality, separate from those around it. Even a pond has components which overlap with the surrounding grassland, woodland, or heathland in which it is situated. Not only will animals such as frogs or dragonflies move between the different systems but leaves will fall in the pond and decay and mineral salts will wash into the pond from the surrounding soil. The ocean systems are, of course, even more closely linked to the many different ecosystems that surround them. So all ecosystems are linked in one way or another and anything which disrupts one system may have far-reaching and hard to predict effects on other ecosystems. All living organisms and their environments are linked to form a thin film on the surface of the Earth which is called the **biosphere**.

Another important idea to understand is that of **habitat**. Within any ecosystem there will be many different 'homes' into which animals and plants fit. These habitats may be quite restricted, such as under stones or in rotting wood for woodlice, or very large, such as the area of grassland occupied by a pride of lions. In every case, however, the habitat will be the place which offers a tolerable range of living conditions for the animals and plants living there. By limiting themselves to a particular habitat, organisms are able to make the best use of the conditions within the ecosystem whilst, at the same time, contributing to the system as a whole.

At first sight it might not seem important if one small habitat is altered, but just imagine a situation where a school cleaner-in-charge or caretaker (or headteacher!) decides to tidy up a piece of waste ground around the school by removing all the stones, rubbish, and bits of rotting wood, etc. This would remove the habitat for the woodlice, who would either die or move elsewhere – perhaps into the caretaker's garden! Now organisms such as centipedes or hedgehogs, which feed on the woodlice, would have to find another source of food or, in turn, move away. The same could apply to some birds so, in a short time, an ecosystem where children could have studied many living things might become an impoverished wasteland, not unlike the 'green deserts' of many school playing fields. This simple example points out how careful we must be before making any changes to a habitat. This is because changes like this may soon affect a whole ecosystem. As we have already noted, ecosystems are all interlinked into the biosphere so the ripples from a habitat change may spread far wider than you think!

Think about the school in which you work. Does this sort of thing happen? Do you have carefully manicured rose gardens at the front entrance of the school as part of an attempt to impress visitors, including prospective parents? Do you lament the loss of birdlife in the immediate surroundings of the school buildings? Do the birds, in turn, lament the loss of the insects they used to feed on that gathered in the non-sprayed, pre-rosebush vegetation that once grew around the margins of the school buildings?

The simple example above also serves to draw our attention to another important idea. When we interact with our environment, unlike woodlice or birds, we can make decisions in which we weigh up the pros and cons of alternative courses of action.

How do we balance the needs of the birds themselves against our need for birdlife to be available for study by the children in the school? Is the need for some sort of impressive landscaped garden entrance, suggesting to visitors a sense of formality, purpose, and control and expressing a value system about education, of more value to the school than a wildlife area? Do rose gardens mean more pupils in the school and teachers keeping their jobs? In terms of balance, it really depends on your perspective!

SO WHAT IS 'ECOLOGY'?

In order to more fully explore the interrelations within ecosystems we will take just one example and examine in detail how the major physical and biotic factors impinge on the lives of the organisms living there. We could take any ecosystem to do this but, since it is one with which many of us may be familiar, we have chosen to examine the woodland ecosystem.

When you look at a woodland the first thing you notice is the trees! On closer examination you may well find that a particular type of tree occupies most of the space and this then represents the *dominant* species in the ecosystem. This dominant species will have a major impact upon the nature of the ecosystem. Thus we can readily see the difference between an oak woodland, a beech woodland, and a fir woodland. The latter two types of woodland are dominated by trees which have closely packed leaves and

which, as a consequence, produce an area beneath them of deep shade, where
leaves of the oak are arranged so as to allow a large area of lighter shade bene[...]
trees. Let us examine the implications of this further.

In any ecosystem the greatest mass of living material – called the **biomass** – will
consist of green plants. This may not be as obvious in the case of a pond or the ocean
but, for an ecosystem to function, this must be the case. To see why this is we need to
examine the relationships between the components of our ecosystem further.

All the green plants in our woodland are able to make their own food from carbon
dioxide gas, water, and mineral salts. The carbon dioxide gas is present in the air and is
absorbed through small pores in the leaves, called **stomata**. The water and mineral salts
are absorbed from the soil by the roots. Water and carbon dioxide are no use as a food
source so these plants have a sophisticated mechanism for combining these two simple
chemicals to form sugar.

Water + Carbon dioxide ⟶ **Sugar + Oxygen**

Sugar is a common natural store of energy. Storage of sugar in plants, however, is
difficult as it is soluble, so it is often quickly converted to insoluble starch.

Probably the chemical reactions we are most familiar with are ones in which energy
is *released*. Activities like burning wood or petrol release energy as heat and the original
complex chemicals are broken down into simpler ones in these processes. You will not
be surprised, then, to hear that combining simple chemicals into more complex ones
requires an *input* of energy and, in the case of our green plants, the energy to do this
comes from light. Green plants are green because they contain a complex material
called chlorophyll which is able to 'trap' light energy and then use this energy to cause
the carbon dioxide and water to combine. This is the process known as
photosynthesis.

Any organism which can use energy to synthesize its food is called an **autotroph** and
some other living things, notably some bacteria, can use energy sources other than light
to do this. However the most important mechanism for converting simple chemicals
into usable foodstuff remains photosynthesis.

All living things need a supply of energy to make their bodies work. This is not only
for obvious things, such as animals like us moving around. Energy is also needed to
drive all the chemical reactions which enable us to grow, digest our food, and even
think. Plants are no different from animals in needing energy to drive the chemical
processes in their bodies and, although they don't run about, they do need plenty of
energy to grow. Just think how much energy it must have taken to grow a large tree!
After all, if you cut it down and burnt it, you would get a pretty hot bonfire!

In order to obtain the energy they need, plants break down some of the stored starch
back to water and carbon dioxide. Although this takes place all the time, when light is
available photosynthesis is working and immediately uses up this carbon dioxide. Thus
it is only at night that the carbon dioxide from respiration is released to the atmosphere.
During the day plants work at an energy surplus. They take in more energy than they
need to live and the excess is available to support life at night and for growth.

In the light, far more oxygen is produced than the plant needs for its respiration, so
much oxygen is released. Throughout the whole biosphere the amount of oxygen
released by plants compensates for the oxygen used by animals, so that the balance of

carbon dioxide and oxygen is more or less constant in the atmosphere. If the ratio of plants to animals were to change significantly the effect on living things would be very serious. Also, if we burn large quantities of plant-derived material we replace that oxygen with carbon dioxide. Burning fossil fuels thus replaces oxygen produced in prehistoric times with yet more carbon dioxide. There is some evidence that in ancient times the atmosphere was richer in carbon dioxide and that this situation was progressively modified by the expansion of the plant kingdom. As we shall see later, this situation has been reversed in more recent times by human activity.

Starch forms a very convenient energy store for plants but for growth and development many other materials are required. This is where mineral salts are used. Among the most important elements supplied by these mineral salts are nitrogen, phosphorus, and potassium. If you look at a packet of general garden fertilizer you will see that these three elements are present in the largest quantities. To build up the plant's body structure many different substances must be synthesized but the largest bulk will be protein to build the basic structure of the cells. On your garden fertilizer packet you may find other elements listed such as iron and magnesium, but these will be in smaller quantities.

If you consider a plant living in an artificial situation, in a pot inside a house, you will appreciate that the plant will soon suffer if it is short of water or not placed in the light. Poor growth or effects such as yellowing of the leaves often indicate that the soil has become short of mineral salts and this is where the application of some fertilizer or 'plant feed' is called for. In our natural ecosystem, the woodland, these effects are rarely seen. Certainly there will be few, if any, plants growing under the deep shade of a fir or beech tree and even under an oak tree most of the plants beneath its shade will be straggly and weak compared to those growing in full sunlight. Some plants, such as ivy or valerian, do thrive in the shaded region and thus are protected from competition from plants such as rosebay willowherb, which can only grow in bright sunlight.

This provides us with a good example of biotic factors at work in the environment. The smaller plants are competing with the taller trees for light and this is controlling the distribution of these smaller plants. Light is, however, only one of the factors controlling the distribution of plants.

Under fir trees we find that few if any green plants can survive, yet surely some plants can grow in deep shade? Some types of ivy and some ferns grow in very deep shade successfully, yet they cannot grow under fir trees. The reason is that the fir trees have shallow roots and remove much of the water from the upper layer of soil thus making the soil too dry for other plants to survive. In addition, the soil under fir trees becomes very acidic, another factor which many other plants cannot tolerate. The situation under the fully developed canopy of beech trees is very similar, yet early in the year you will find plants such as wood anemone, dog's mercury, and cuckoo pint growing well. Unlike the fir trees, beech trees are deciduous so there is a period before the canopy develops when smaller plants can develop – if they are quick enough! Although green plants do not grow well under fir and beech this does not apply to non-green plants, the fungi. They live on dead organic matter, such as fallen leaves, and require little water, so the dark, dry conditions under fir and beech are very suitable for fungal growth.

There are, of course, very few areas of truly natural woodland left in Europe. We and our ancestors have cut away or managed woodlands for hundreds of years and one common practice has been to remove the larger trees for timber leaving the smaller ones to grow on. This results in the sudden production of patches of light where rain can make the soil damp and where small plants can quickly establish themselves. Even what may look superficially like a very natural ecosystem is likely on closer examination to reveal the effects of human intervention.

On the face of it this particular example of intervention seems benign. The opening up of the woodland has let in a whole new group of flowering plants. To be certain of this, however, we must look beyond the plants.

In any ecosystem there will be a range of animals, herbivores, which feed on the plants. Feeding on these herbivores will be other animals, carnivores.

Plants⟶ Herbivores⟶ Carnivores

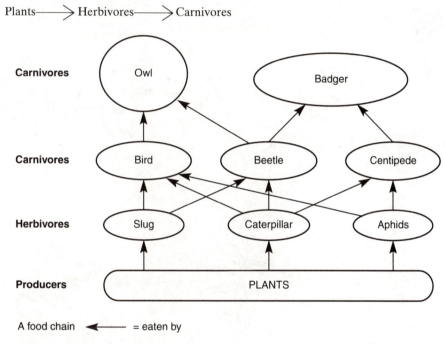

Figure 1.2   *Food chains*

This constitutes a simple food chain (see Figure 1.2). However, in our woodland example there would be many types of herbivores: aphids, caterpillars, slugs, etc. feeding on the plants; and many types of carnivores, for example, beetles, centipedes, birds feeding on the herbivores; and bigger carnivores, for example, owls, badgers, feeding on them. So, there will be many food chain lines, not just one. Thus, in reality, there is rarely anything as simple as a chain but there is rather a food web, as seen in Figure 1.3.

If any one component of such a web is removed then the other members of the web may have to adjust their feeding patterns, or they will die out. So long as organisms can make use of alternative sources of food this adjustment is usually possible, although it may increase competition for the remaining food sources. If, say, a herbivore can only utilize one species of plant then its position is far more precarious. This is the case with koala bears in Australia, which feed exclusively on eucalyptus leaves.

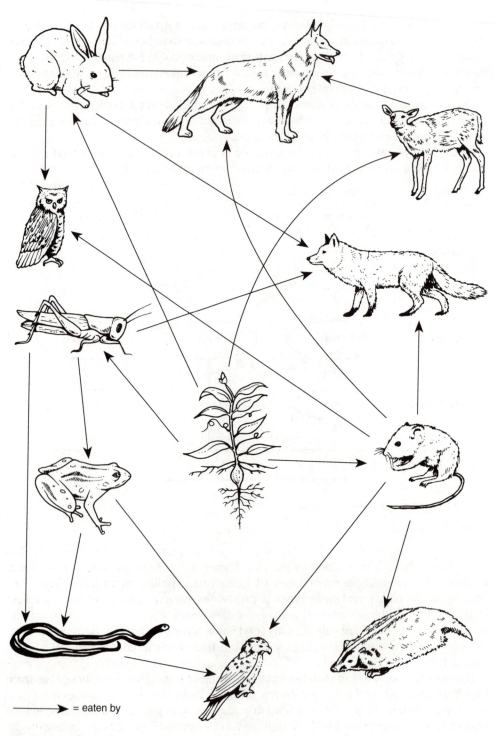

→ = eaten by

Figure 1.3   *A food web*

Opening up the woodland to allow in new plants will also allow in new types of herbivores and carnivores which may well upset the balance and perhaps drive some original species out whilst allowing some new species to become pests.

The food web gives only a very limited view of the relationships within an ecosystem. A more useful idea is that of the **biomass pyramid**. The reason for using biomass rather than numbers is fairly obvious in a woodland. There are not a great number of trees, but they form the greatest mass. It is also probably obvious that there are a great many more insects of one sort or another than there are owls. The ecologist would need to find the biomass of each feeding level, by estimating their numbers then multiplying this by the mass of the average individual.

A pyramid of biomass can be obtained by plotting the biomass of each feeding level as shown in figure 1.4 below. This method of illustrating the feeding relationships in an ecosystem can be done for any ecosystem and, although differing in detail, the overall shape of the pyramid would be similar.

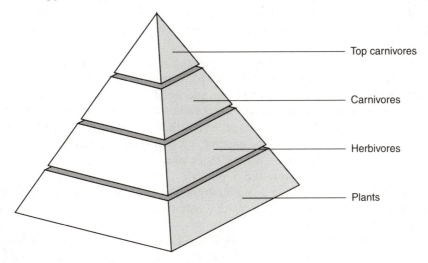

Top carnivores

Carnivores

Herbivores

Plants

Figure 1.4   *A pyramid of biomass*

You may be wondering why this shape is a pyramid. Well, the use of food is never 100 per cent efficient, in fact the efficiency is usually only about 30 per cent, so a far bigger mass of plants is needed than the mass of animals feeding on them. This applies all the way up the pyramid so there are usually relatively few large animals at the top of the pyramid.

For example, if you go on a safari holiday you will be lucky to see any lions as their numbers are so low, yet you will see large numbers of antelope and other herbivores on which the lions feed. We, of course, are the exception to this general rule! How this has come about, and how this top-heavy situation can be maintained will be dealt with shortly.

In terms of our teaching, children will find the notion of a food chain easier to handle than a food web as a means of looking at feeding relationships within an ecosystem. As is so often the case, it is the raising of questions through interaction with our surroundings that can lead to understanding.

In a school context, children may have seen families of, say, rabbits grazing a grassy hillside. This food chain is fairly direct in terms of grass, of which there is much, rabbits, who can be seen scampering away from their grazing lands when we disturb them, and foxes, which we tend to see alone and rarely. Classroom discussion of other food chains can develop from ideas on the initiation of most chains via the consumption of green plants. For some children, the notion of food webs will become apparent when they begin to consider multiple predators and food sources. The provision of sort cards with illustrations of common plants and animals on them is an excellent way of enabling children to explore green plant food sources and prey–predator relationships. It helps build up an awareness of food webs and, for just a few children, may begin to indicate the nature of a biomass pyramid.

The plants at the base of a biomass pyramid are strongly affected by anything which changes their light, water or mineral supply. Each stratum of the pyramid requires more of the layer below it to survive. We can appreciate that a small change affecting the lower levels can have disastrous effects on the top level. Since *we* are at the top level of so many pyramids the danger of upsetting the balance lower down should be easily appreciated!

So far we have concentrated upon the passage of food material up the pyramid. There is generally no shortage of carbon dioxide or light but, as we saw with house plants, minerals do get used up in the soil and need replenishment if plants are to continue to grow in that soil. In a balanced ecosystem this is no problem. As plants and animals die their bodies fall onto the soil where they are broken down by fungi and bacteria in the process of decay. The minerals used in synthesizing their proteins and other body materials are broken down to simple mineral salts which can then be taken up by the roots of the next generation of plants.

There are many such processes going on in the soil, each releasing various components but, since nitrogen is so important, we illustrate in Figure 1.5 just one such cycle, that which returns nitrogen to the soil.

These cycles are self-sustaining so long as this circular pattern is not interrupted in any way, for example by removing some link. Unfortunately, many of our activities do just this, forestry and agriculture being two major examples which we will examine in detail later.

In a natural ecosystem the balance of all the components is maintained by the existence of limiting factors. Thus in our woodland example the balance of the different plant species was determined by competition for light, water, and space, and this in turn would limit the size of the various animal populations. If, for example, a species of caterpillar became too abundant and ate all the leaves of its food plant, then it would die out and the plants would recover.

Another limiting factor in an ecosystem can be the buildup of toxic materials. Since all the chemical reactions going on in living organisms, which we call their **metabolic processes**, are so complex, some of the by-products are of no use and may even be harmful. These waste products are either voided as soon as possible, as in most animals, or are stored in a harmless insoluble form until they can be got rid of. For example, many plant waste products are shed with the old leaves in most plants. If these toxins were to build up in the soil they would eventually poison the organisms living there and destroy the ecosystem. However, in the soil there are a whole range of bacteria and

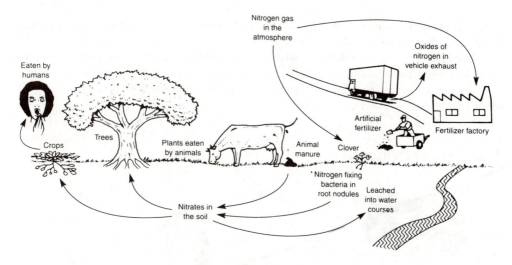

Figure 1.5 *The nitrogen cycle*

fungi which live on these waste materials and, in doing so, break them down to water, carbon dioxide, and mineral salts.

If toxins enter the soil which are 'foreign' then there will not be any bacteria or fungi able to break them down. These toxins may be taken up by the plants, and in turn enter the herbivores and finally the top carnivores. Because each herbivore eats a great amount of plants and each carnivore a large number of herbivores the amount of toxins in the body will increase as you move up the pyramid. So a pesticide used to kill aphids may reach such a high concentration by the time it gets into sparrow hawks that they will be poisoned by it. So, it is not only what we take out of a balanced ecosystem which needs to be controlled, but also what may be put into it!

You will remember that we have stressed the essential interrelatedness of ecosystems. If, by either exclusion or inclusion of materials an ecosystem is destroyed, then this will probably adversely affect neighbouring ecosystems. This raises the very real danger of setting in train a 'domino' effect whereby increasing numbers of ecosystems collapse until the whole biosphere is threatened.

Fortunately ecosystems, like the bodies of individual organisms, display a strong tendency to the process called **homeostasis**. This is the process by which changes to one part of a system are cancelled out by changes to another so that the overall equilibrium is maintained. A simple example is the temperature control mechanism in your body. When you get too hot you perspire and the evaporation of this thin film of body surface water cools you back down to the correct temperature. Similarly the body can cope with toxins by increasing the rate of toxin metabolism and excretion. This is what happens when someone has imbibed too much alcohol. The rate of alcohol breakdown in the liver is increased and the rate at which the kidneys excrete the products of the breakdown is also increased. In a relatively short time the body has eliminated the toxin and returns to normal. Similar mechanisms operate in ecosystems but, just like homeostatic processes in the body, there are limits. If your body temperature rises too high then you may die. Similarly, too high a concentration of alcohol in the blood will be fatal. The situation is worse when a toxin which cannot be metabolized enters the body; the results are quickly fatal. Again the same applies to an ecosystem when a toxin enters which cannot be broken down.

Although only a brief outline of a very complex situation, we hope that you now have sufficient information about the basic mechanisms of ecosystem maintenance to enable you to apply this knowledge to the more detailed examination of environmental problems in later chapters.

LOOKING AT OUR PAST

Figure 1.6 *'Oh dear – another sci-fi film!'*

To understand how many of our present problems with the environment have come about we need to examine the development of our ancestors in relation to their environment.

So far as we can determine, our forebears were 'hunter-gatherers'. They lived in small bands and roamed over quite large areas collecting edible plants and killing such animals as they could with their primitive weapons. These people were almost certainly nomadic. When a favoured food source became difficult to find they simply moved on to another area where it was still plentiful. This way of life would have been unlikely to result in the elimination of any food species, whether animal or plant, because they would have moved when the food source became difficult to find easily, not when it was exhausted entirely. Once the band had moved on, then the food species would have been able to regain their original numbers, by the homeostatic mechanism. In addition, such waste as the human band left behind would then be subject to the natural processes of decay without becoming a toxic mass of critical proportions.

This way of life probably persisted for tens of thousands of years and, during this time, the total human population of the Earth was probably about eight million, which is less than the present population of one large city such as London! Humans were thus unlikely to disturb the ecological balance so long as their numbers did not become too great and as long as they were not confined to a restricted location for a long period of time.

Problems could arise when one band encroached upon the territory of another since this would lead to competition for food. It seems probable that the tribal rivalries, so common between even so-called 'civilized' different human groups today, may have originated in his way.

One way to limit such conflicts and to ensure a more reliable food supply was to collect potential meat-yielding animals together into a herd so that they could be protected from other carnivores and their breeding be encouraged. This way of life is still seen in a few groups, such as the Lapps with their herds of reindeer. However, this approach still requires a nomadic existence since the animals must be allowed to wander in search of food as they reduce supplies in an area.

More people could be supported, however, if they could stay in one place and the way to achieve this was to develop agriculture. The cultivation of crops could allow groups to stay in one place and provide food for both themselves and their animals. This more reliable food supply would allow the size of a population to increase further which would, in turn, require an expansion in the area of cultivated land. This expansion could, of course, eventually lead to territorial conflicts with neighbouring groups, thus limiting both further expansion and mobility. One obvious solution to this problem was improvement in agricultural techniques so that the same amount of land would yield greatly increased amounts of food.

As a result of these developments, by about 2,000 years ago the population of the Earth is estimated to have increased about 40 times, to reach a total of 300 million. So, for many thousands of years before the development of agriculture the human population had remained fairly stable. Yet in the next 8,000 years this vast increase had taken place. The reason was, of course, that the limiting factors of the early humans' natural ecosystem had been removed by developments in agriculture.

It is in studying evidence of some of these early farming communities that archae-ologists have uncovered evidence of environmental conflict. The problem was that increased productivity from a limited area of land could only be sustained so long as the fertility of the land remained high. As soon as the nutrients and humus were depleted from the soil, productivity would fall and the group would be forced to move on. One of the consequences of this would be that trees would be removed to expand the area of cultivable land. Of course, as populations grew, trees would also be useful for making dwellings and tools and for use as a fuel. It is important to appreciate that the 'slash and burn' approach to land clearance in South America and South East Asia today which causes such concern is not a new phenomenon. Human groups have been doing this for many thousands of years and, as a result, the tree cover all over the Earth has been declining. In fact, many of the great deserts of the globe have almost certainly arisen as a result of agricultural practices in the past.

So the idea of our ancestors living in harmony with the environment and doing it no harm is almost certainly a myth. By contrast the evidence is that, once the hunter-gatherer way of life was superseded by a more settled existence, environmental damage was the norm rather than the exception. Once humans had learned how to remove the limiting factors on their population growth, then conflict with a stable ecosystem structure was inevitable.

Why then is it only in relatively recent time that environmental concerns have become news? One of the key factors is another side effect of moving from a nomadic to a settled way of life. Greater efficiency of food production resulted in fewer people being needed to work the land, thus releasing people for other activities. This increased food production led to increased urbanization and to the growth of towns and cities. The increased population, in turn, required even greater food production with the consequent increasing danger of exhausting the land. To a degree this could be met by using the waste from animals to return needed nutrients to the soil and by crop rotation. Eventually, however, the only way such concentrations could survive was by importing food and other materials from further afield and thus these conurbations became dependent upon improved transportation. We mentioned earlier how small, nomadic bands could easily dispose of their waste. In large towns this now became a problem which historically was dealt with by dumping the waste outside the towns or by burying it where the natural processes of decay would, over time, return nutrients to the soil.

So far, so good, but then came industrialization! Early industries were small-scale and catered for local needs. Pottery, weaving, metal working all used up some natural resources and produced waste, some of which would decay very slowly. It is from these ancient waste pits containing pieces of pottery and metal implements that we can find out much about early settlements. Undoubtedly the furnaces and kilns did release some pollutants into the atmosphere and into the rivers. However the scale of the problem was such that it had little impact on the vastness of the global environment.

The real problem of industrial pollution began in Britain in the eighteenth century but soon spread into Europe and the rest of the 'developed' world. It is ironic that, just as the developed world is becoming aware of and concerned about the effects of pollution, the spread of industrialization into developing countries threatens a massive increase in the scale of this problem. Undoubtedly, it was industrialization which brought wealth and political power to the countries of the developed world but with it came many problems.

We have already mentioned population growth in early communities but, since the Industrial Revolution, the problem has become far more serious. For example, the world population in 1650 was estimated to be about 500 million, whereas in 1986 it had increased to 4,750 million. By 2025, at the present rate of increase, it could be ten billion, by the end of the twenty-first century 40 billion, and by 2350 four *trillion*: four million million. Surely these numbers are too large for most of us to comprehend? This increase in population has, in most countries, gone hand in hand with a further increase in urbanization to the point where, in Great Britain, more than 80 per cent of the population now live in towns.

To support such large urban populations there is an ever-increasing demand for more food, more energy, and all the material requirements of urban society. In addition, as fewer people are required to provide for the needs of the community more time becomes available for recreational activities. These requirements place great pressures on the environment outside the towns in a variety of ways and in subsequent chapters we will examine in detail the problems created.

We can summarize the problems we have identified as follows:

- Land is made over to agriculture with the consequent loss of other ecosystems, especially forests and wetlands. The loss of trees has serious knock-on effects on both soil and the atmosphere.
- Intensive farming cannot be supported by simply returning organic matter such as manure to the soil to replenish depleted minerals, so artificial fertilizers are used.
- Excess artificial fertilizers are leached through the soil and enter the water table.
- Raw materials to supply industry are mined or quarried thus destroying further natural ecosystems.
- The transport of food and materials for industry requires the development of roads and railways which destroy further areas of countryside.
- The waste products of urban populations and of industry are frequently composed of materials for which no decay-producing bacteria exist. The dumps of waste thus destroy further ecosystems. There is a limit to the amount of waste the biosphere can accommodate.
- Soluble, toxic waste may be leached into the water table.
- Towns and industry require large energy supplies, most of which are derived from fossil fuels.
- The burning of fossil fuels and other industrial processes produce atmospheric pollutants some of which may be washed back to the surface as toxic substances whilst others remain to change the composition of the air.
- Although scientists cannot agree on a time scale, all accept that the current rate of population growth cannot be supported indefinitely by the biosphere. Either some control over this expansion must be exercised or natural homeostatic mechanisms, operating through famine, conflicts, or disease will impose a limitation on further growth.

Chapter 2

The Staff of Life

In Chapter 1 we referred to an estimate that, by the end of the twenty-first century, the population of our Earth could reach 40 billion. Obtaining food in sufficient quantity and variety will always be a key factor in the survival of any animal species and we are no exception. So how can we hope to obtain sufficient food to satisfy the needs of such vast numbers?

FEEDING THE FORTY BILLION

Figure 2.1 *'I'll need more than a few loaves and fishes to pull off this one!'*

In terms of their food requirements, animals can be categorized as herbivores, which eat only plants, carnivores which eat only animals, and omnivores, which eat both. On this categorization we are omnivores. Both herbivores and carnivores have specialized feeding and digestive systems to enable them to make the best use of their chosen food source.

Herbivores are adapted to cope with the tough cellulose walls of plant cells by having some teeth which are sharp enough to cut through the plant stems and others which are able to grind the plant material so finely that the cells are split open. Much of the nutrient value of plants comes from within the cells, so breaking these open is essential. For many herbivores, such as cattle, the bulk of their food will be grass which consists largely of cellulose which animals cannot digest. To overcome this problem animals such as cows have an additional compartment in their digestive tract in which they harbour a rich population of cellulose-digesting bacteria. In return for providing the bacteria with a comfortable home and finding food for them the cow receives all the products of cellulose digestion that the bacteria do not require. Because a diet of grass or similar plant material is very low in protein, animals relying on such a diet must eat almost continually to survive. Herbivores which can make use of some richer sources of protein, as found in some nuts and berries, thus have an advantage. Many herbivores, like the koala bear, are so specialized that they can only feed on a single species of plant. This degree of specialization is fine so long as the plant food is available. Should anything happen to destroy the plant in a particular area then the specialized herbivore must either move to find a new source of food or it too will die out. Any change in the environment which eliminates a particular plant species may thus also wipe out any animals dependent upon that plant.

Carnivores are also specialized to make the best use of their food source. They also have cutting teeth at the front of the mouth to slice off pieces of flesh but also have pointed teeth which may be used to tear open a carcass or to kill their prey. Behind these are usually teeth arranged like scissors which are able to cut off pieces of flesh and behind these again powerful, flatter teeth which are effective for crushing hard material such as bones, the shells of molluscs, or the hard coverings of insects.

Carnivores are rarely so specialized in their diet as herbivores, most being able to eat nearly anything they manage to catch. Since an all-meat diet may be deficient in some vitamins, especially vitamin C, many carnivores are capable of eating a limited amount of plant material. Complete carnivores must, however, make use of every part of their prey and so must have powerful digestive systems which can cope with bones, fur, and insect coverings as well as flesh. The carnivore diet is generally much more nutritious than that of herbivores and thus they eat far less frequently and, when young, have time for play activities during which they learn the skills required to catch their food. Although less susceptible to these difficulties than some herbivores, carnivores can easily be threatened if a major food source is lost.

Omnivores have much less specialized feeding and digestive systems than herbivores or even carnivores. Consequently they cannot, for example, digest cellulose or make full use of materials such as bone and fur. On the other hand, their lack of specialization means that, should one source of food dry up, they can easily change to another and so are generally less susceptible to food shortages arising from environmental changes. If omnivores are forced out of an area by factors such as competition or water shortage they are more likely to be able to adapt to a new situation than the more specialized herbivores or carnivores. This adaptability is one of the factors which has enabled us humans to live in a wide variety of different environments and make use of whatever food source happened to be available.

The early hunter-gatherers were able to obtain their supplies of high quality or 'first-class' protein, fats, minerals, and vitamins from the animals they killed and to supplement this with plant material rich in carbohydrates as well as other minerals and vitamins. Thus a nutritious diet was available which gave them time for non-feeding activities. The development of agriculture provided a more readily available source of all the components of a balanced diet and so provided even more free time, so long as the land remained productive and there was adequate rainfall. Where land is, or has become, less productive through over-use, then the value of feeding animals as well as growing plants may be called into question. Thus, if cattle are fed on grain, it takes about ten kilograms of grain to produce one kilogram of beef. Unless there is plenty of free grassland to feed the animals on then it may seem preferable to eat the ten kilograms of grain directly! Whilst this approach might increase the quantity of food available, it could have serious implications for the quality of that diet since meat is a better source of high-quality protein, of certain essential fats, and some vitamins and minerals, such as zinc.

Although by-passing the meat stage appears attractive, an all-cereal diet is deficient in many essential elements and requires a far greater intake of food to produce the same amount of essential protein as would a small amount of meat. Thus in many developing countries the result of an inadequate cereal diet is serious malnutrition.

In developed countries with access to a wide range of alternative foodstuffs a vegetarian diet is a perfectly healthy alternative to eating meat. In these countries there is no shortage of dairy products and eggs which are high in first-class protein and there are also higher protein alternatives to cereals, such as soya. Any missing minerals and vitamins can be replaced by using food supplements. A vegan diet, however, in which no animal products, including milk and milk products, are eaten can only be sustained by healthy adults and is not suitable for growing children, pregnant women, or those with serious illness. This is simply because our omnivorous digestive system is not adapted to extract all the required components of food from plants as would be the case with that of a herbivore.

Before leaving the question of alternative diets it should be mentioned that many human groups established themselves by the sea or by large inland lakes in order to make use of fish as a food source. Where this has happened the diet is always a very good one as fish alone can provide almost all our food requirements. The only possible dietary problem with an all-fish diet (apart from boredom!) would be a shortage of vitamin C. However communities where fish was a major food source usually had access to plant foods as well. The exception to this would be some races living in the Arctic whose diet consists almost entirely of fish and seal meat. This merely serves to underline just how adaptable humans can be in terms of dietary requirements.

FARMING TYPES

Farming can be seen to exist in essentially three types: pastoral farms, where only animals are reared, arable farms, where only crops are grown, and mixed farms where both animals and plants are kept. Pastoral farming tends to be concentrated in upland areas with high rainfall giving lush pasture whereas arable farms tend to be more in drier, lowland areas.

In terms of modifying the environment the 'typical' pastoral farm would seem to be the least destructive. Close cropping of the plants does limit the growth of taller species and leads to the development of typical pastureland with grasses and low-growing meadow flowering plants. It is only when the number of grazing animals becomes too high for the grazing range allowed that over-grazing occurs. This results in sparse, coarse vegetation with areas of bare soil which, because it is no longer bound by the plant roots, is prone to erosion. Initially this erosion is by water but, if the soil then becomes dry, also by wind. When such over-grazing has occurred over a large area the reduced evaporation of water through plant transpiration can begin to affect the local climate so that rainfall is reduced. In extreme cases this can eventually lead to the formation of deserts.

In general, arable farming is likely to lead to more immediate environmental damage. The first and most basic reason for this is that the harvesting of crops necessarily results in the removal of material from the natural ecosystem cycles of renewal. In many cases, however, especially in the case of cereal crops, the amount of material being removed for food is relatively small. If only the seed is removed and the rest of the plant material ploughed back into the soil, arable land can continue being productive for long periods with relatively little input of additional fertilizers or manure. Unfortunately, it is common practice in many countries to burn the stubble after harvesting in order to save labour on ploughing and also to destroy 'weeds' and 'sterilize' the soil. Although this process will still return the minerals contained in the stubble to the soil it will not replace the humus which helps maintain soil structure. Humus is produced from the initial stages of the decay of organic matter in the soil and is a rather structureless, almost jelly-like substance (a **colloid**) which has a great capacity for holding water and dissolved mineral salts. As this humus is broken down by bacteria it slowly releases further nutrients into the soil, especially those containing nitrogen, phosphorus, potassium, and iron. If a soil is deficient in humus then soluble mineral salts will be quickly washed down by rainwater to lower levels where they are inaccessible to plant roots. This process is known as leaching. In fact a number of countries, including the United Kingdom, have now banned the process of stubble burning so this is one disadvantage of arable farming which may become of reduced significance in the future.

Even without stubble burning the continual growth of cereal crops on land cannot be maintained at levels which give high crop yields without the use of added artificial fertilizers. The basic problem with such fertilizers is that they are soluble and so subject to leaching if the soil does not contain much humus and so has poor water retention, or to 'run-off' if they are not quickly absorbed into the soil. Although some modern fertilizers are designed to be less soluble and so are released into the soil more slowly the problem of leaching and run-off is still apparent.

In fact the major problem with the use of artificial fertilizers is that they are frequently used incorrectly. If too much is used, and especially if it is used when the plants are not most actively taking up minerals for growth, then much of the chemical will be leached away. With careful application of just as much chemical as the plants can use during their most active growth phase this loss can be minimized and the effect on crop yield maximized. To achieve this however requires skilled workers and regular soil testing – neither of which are to be found on the majority of farms in developing countries.

Eventually these substances will enter watercourses as pollutants and once they enter streams, rivers, or lakes they can become a serious hazard. This is especially true of nitrogen and phosphorus compounds which encourage the rapid growth of certain freshwater algae. These are small, simple plants which can, nevertheless, multiply rapidly to produce a large mass of plant material in a very short time. Not only do these dense algal 'blooms' stifle the growth of other plants but, as they die, the bacteria responsible for their decay use up all the available oxygen in the water, a process called **eutrophication**. When this happens all animal life from water fleas to fish will be killed and the water will become a foul-smelling, dead sewer. In many places the encroachment of run-off agricultural chemicals into drinking water has become a health hazard and water companies may have to spend vast sums on equipment to remove these unwanted materials.

Excess fertilizers put on arable land can be a hazard, but pesticides and herbicides may prove to be even more hazardous. Because these chemicals are synthetic they have no natural bacteria to break them down and will tend to accumulate in the soil from year to year. Again these substances will eventually leach through into watercourses where they may directly poison animals and plants living in the water and may also enter drinking water. Although the use of the most hazardous and persistent chemicals such as DDT and Lindane have long been banned these chemicals have entered food pyramids and thus become concentrated many times in the bodies of animals towards the top of these pyramids. Although modern pesticides and herbicides are less persistent in the environment, the potential dangers inherent in their continued use should never be underestimated.

Another feature of arable farming is the increased degree of mechanization. Humans started by digging the soil by hand, moved on to hand-driven ploughs and then to the use of horses or oxen. Even with the use of heavy horses the area of hoof placed on the soil was a small proportion of the total area ploughed and the hoof prints were scattered. With the advent of the tractor much greater weights are placed on the soil and the rolling effect of the wheels compacts the soil far more than a human's foot or horse's hoof ever could. To demonstrate this one needs only to observe the effect of pressing down on some dough or clay with the fingers and then compare this with the use of a rolling pin. The increased power made available by the use of tractors also allowed much deeper ploughing which tends to bring more of the sub-soil to the surface.

The combined effect of the techniques of arable farming will tend to damage the structure of the soil. Soil is made up of ground-up and weathered rock particles – the mineral component – combined with bits of decaying organic matter and humus. The humus in particular causes the mineral particles to stick together into clumps, known as soil 'crumbs'. Between these relatively large soil crumbs there will be air spaces. This structure is essential for successful seed germination and root growth in a soil. Both seeds and roots require oxygen from air to respire, an adequate supply of water, and a moderate temperature. Seeds will not germinate nor roots grow in a soil which is too dry, which lacks oxygen, or is too cold. In addition, the growing plant requires a ready supply of essential mineral salts in solution. In a soil with a good structure the oxygen supply is maintained in the spaces between the soil crumbs. Within the crumbs, water and mineral salts are retained. Excess water can drain away through the large spaces between the crumbs without taking too much of the dissolved mineral salts with it. Wet soil remains cold longer in early spring than drier soil.

Thus we can see that a soil whose structure has been damaged by heavy machinery will become less productive unless steps are taken to remedy this situation, usually by adding extra humus from sources such as farmyard manure or seaweed. However, if such purely arable farms are in areas well away from pastoral farms then such organic matter will have to be transported, a process which is inconvenient, expensive, and wasteful of valuable energy resources.

The most modern tractors using 'balloon' tyres, which spread the load over a much larger area of soil, should do much to alleviate the problems of soil compaction but such machinery is expensive and least likely to be available to the farmers in poorer countries where it is most needed.

A further problem with arable farming resulting from the use of large machinery is the removal of hedges to produce very large, open fields. Not only does this practice remove an important ecosystem entirely but the resulting large fields are far more susceptible to erosion by both wind and water.

These problems are, of course, made worse when the soil structure is poor. The problem of fluvial erosion in large fields is far worse when the fields are on a slope, especially when the field is ploughed up and down the slope. Under these circumstances heavy rainfall can result in massive loss of topsoil. By the simple process of using contour ploughing, where the plough is taken across the slope following the contours of the land, the amount of soil erosion can be dramatically reduced. Undoubtedly, however, the better solution is to leave existing hedges or replace those which have been removed. Not only does this reduce the problems of erosion but the animals in the hedgerow community play an important role in keeping down pests and diseases which would otherwise damage the crops and would thus need to be controlled using pesticides and herbicides.

From what has been said above it would seem that mixed farming practices represent a better approach and in large measure this is true. In a mixed farming economy there will be a readily available supply of manure from the animals which can be used to maintain the fertility and structure of the soil without the use of large quantities of artificial fertilizers. The organic matter will decay naturally in the soil to form humus and maintain the soil structure.

It is often suggested that a return to 'old-fashioned' farming techniques in which only natural fertilizer, in the form of farmyard manure, is used would solve all the problems of modern farming. However, before the use of artificial fertilizers, pesticides, and herbicides, the productivity of farms in Great Britain at the beginning of the twentieth century was only one sixth of that today. In addition, it needs to be appreciated that even farmyard manure, if used in too large quantities, still produces large amounts of soluble nitrogen and phosphorus salts which through leaching and run-off can pollute the watercourses just as badly as artificial fertilizers. If, however, the balance between animals and crops on a mixed farm is appropriate then a more balanced farming ecosystem may be established in many areas. In other places, such as uplands, the most appropriate agriculture will be the rearing of cattle, sheep, deer, and goats which can graze on grass and by doing so enhance rather than detract from the environment.

We need food. In order to support our large populations, agriculture is a necessary means of food production, yet this needs to be achieved with minimal damage to the environment. A balance has to be achieved between producing sufficient food for the population and using the minimum amount of land without causing pollution so that as many natural ecosystems as possible are retained. To do this the agricultural land must be farmed as intensively as possible, using all available modern techniques to minimize the impact of agriculture on the natural environment. This is a task which will not be achieved by the hit and miss methods of the past. It requires the active participation of a knowledgeable and understanding public. The best place to start this process is surely in the primary school.

Let us take an example from primary schools to illustrate this point. Language plays a vital role in understanding. Part of that understanding relates back to attitudes to our surroundings and the value systems we develop.

Have you noticed in schools, for example, that children will often refer to soil as 'dirt'? This is a really unfortunate misuse of the term. Clearly it derives from children playing outside, coming into contact with the ground and becoming dirty. So it is that perhaps this breeds the misconception that soil is just 'dirt' – that is something not very nice that discolours clothing and bodies. This notion has become so ingrained that dirty items are often referred to as being 'soiled'. On this basis it is hard to develop an appreciation of the value of soil, which after all is fundamental to most of our food production!

More generally, to redress the balance, children need exposure to the increasing number of 'visitor farms' that are springing up on the margins of large cities. These help to provide the concrete link between food production and consumption so that children have an awareness of agricultural products such as milk beyond the fluorescent glare of the refrigerated supermarket shelves!

Of course, learning about our interaction with soil and animals need not just be the province of visits beyond the school gates. This may in itself cultivate another misconception that valued landscapes and practices are always somewhere else and not in our immediate locality. Virtually any primary school setting can provide facilities for children to grow and care for things. Window boxes, courtyard pots and roof gardens are still available even to inner-city schools. Even better, from this type of activity children will be able not only to observe life cycles, but also to take account of decaying plant material and undertake composting. Rural schools with available land are the clear winners in terms of the diversity of plant life they can maintain. Why not tomato cultivation and pear and apple mini-orchards? Some schools even sell their produce and raise money for school funds!

When children are given a choice of seeds to plant, then cries of 'I don't like that!' are bound to be heard. From this specific school example we can generalize. One of the major problems with feeding people is that food is subject to such extremes of prejudice.

In many of the developing countries there have been great difficulties in getting people to accept new methods of farming and to eat new food crops. If you think about it, would you really be happy with the suggestion that you should eat dogs, rats, or insects? These are all good food sources, yet in our Western culture we find the notion of using them as food repulsive.

Food prejudice is often based not only on tradition, but is compounded by religion. We are all aware that an orthodox Jew would die of starvation rather than eat pork, as would a devout Hindu rather than eat beef. How many of you reading this book would readily accept a transfusion of blood, or even a transplanted organ such as a kidney, liver, or heart from the dead body of another human being? If you were starving, on the other hand, would you be prepared to eat the flesh of a dead human animal? Cannibalism was very common amongst many human tribes in the past, so there seems no biological reason not to eat human flesh.

These food prejudices can cause unexpected problems when attempts are made to improve food sources! For example, it was found that people of Northern Burma were seriously deficient in animal protein, although they did raise a small breed of black pigs. If the yield of these pigs could be improved the problem would be solved. By crossbreeding with another larger strain this was achieved successfully and the new strain was introduced to the farmers. Unfortunately, this new strain of pig was spotted, instead of being all black, and the local people considered spotted pigs to be unfit to eat!

This problem of food prejudice is one which would need to be overcome if another promising proposal was to bear fruit. The types of animals humans commonly use for food are really very limited. Antelope, zebra and, especially, eland are all species of African herd animals which are far better adapted to the local conditions, including drought, than domestic cattle and are far more resistant to many diseases. Why not develop these as food animals rather than spending vast sums of money trying to make cattle survive in an environment to which they are less well suited? There are some movements towards exploiting newer food sources, as shown by the farming of emu in Australia and, more recently, ostrich in Europe.

Fish farming is another under-used source, for this has tended to concentrate on expensive fish such as salmon and trout. The technology learned in these 'fish farms' could, however, be applied to many other parts of the world and to a much wider range of fish species.

So far we have concentrated upon developing food by an extension of traditional means, but we have already used the term 'technology' on more than one occasion. Could this be an answer to the world's food problems?

TECHNOLOGY TO THE RESCUE?

Technology is being seen as a possible method of increasing our food supplies in two main ways.

Firstly, biotechnology has been employed for many years in the improvement of food crops, primarily plants, but also to some degree animals. So what is biotechnology? Well, here are two commonly used definitions:

'The use of biological systems to bring about services and products'
'The application of biological organisms and processes to manufacturing and service industries'.

So processes such as baking, brewing, agriculture, antibiotic manufacture, waste disposal, breeding programmes and genetic engineering would all come under the heading 'biotechnology'.

Perhaps the most famous example of the employment of biotechnology was in the 'Green Revolution' of the early 1970s. This involved the use of modern plant-breeding techniques to develop new strains of high-yielding, short-stemmed varieties of wheat, maize, and rice. These high-yielding varieties were so much more efficient than the native strains grown in developing countries that, particularly in Asia, they moved many countries from a food deficit to a food surplus situation.

Unfortunately, these new varieties required increased irrigation, the use of large inputs of artificial fertilizers and the use of weedkillers and pesticides to protect the crops. Although much more efficient, the cost of growing these crops could only be met by the richer landowners who thus gained greatly from this innovation whilst the poorer tenant farmers gained little or nothing from them. As a result, the 'Green Revolution' has probably simply increased social inequalities by widening the gap between the rich and poor in those countries where it has been used extensively. Further harmful effects have resulted from the indiscriminate use of herbicides and pesticides, for these have entered the watercourses, polluting them and damaging fish stocks and duck herds and even contaminating human water supplies.

Perhaps the greatest benefit to be gained from the 'Green Revolution' was that it warned us of the dangers of using biotechnology without careful analysis of all the likely consequences. Today we have the great advantage that computer models can be constructed to try to predict the outcomes of any innovation. These models allow for the introduction of a wide range of variables and alternate scenarios, thus giving more warning of potential side effects of any change.

One of the key changes in the approach adopted by modern researchers has been to move away from the notion of introducing new crops into areas in favour of trying to improve the existing, hardy crops that grow there. These crops are already adapted to survive harsh conditions of drought and extremes of temperature. The aim of modern biotechnology research is to maintain these characteristics whilst improving both yield and disease resistance.

The key researcher in biotechnology is still the plant breeder but now the application of sophisticated genetic analytical techniques makes possible a much more focused programme. Thus by analysing the genetics of wheat it has been possible to identify the genes needed to give wheat the best bread-making qualities. New varieties can then be bred from plants which display the required genetic structure. By using genetic analysis there have also been some important breakthroughs in developing plants which are disease resistant.

Genetic engineering

A serious disease of tomatoes is the tobacco mosaic virus. By introducing an inert component of that virus into tomato plants they become fully resistant to the live virus. In another example a gene from a bacterium *Bacillus thuringiensis* (the name doesn't matter!) introduced into plants confers resistance to insect attack and thus improves yield without the need to resort to using insecticides. Not only does this approach directly reduce the input of insecticides into the environment, but it solves the problem of having to educate farmers to use the chemicals correctly.

The impact of biotechnology need not, however, stop at producing better plant varieties. One of the major problems of food supplies is that they are frequently produced most successfully far away from the areas where they are needed. Transportation costs are one problem but, even if this can be overcome, the deterioration of food during transport may make the whole process uneconomic. Studies of tomato plants have identified the gene which makes the fruits go soft after picking and it has subsequently been found possible to 'switch off' the gene responsible for this. Thus the tomatoes can be transported long distances without going soft and without the use of any chemicals or refrigeration methods which would spoil the fruit for the consumer.

These are simple examples of genetic engineering and, although such developments are really still in their infancy, the potential of this research is obviously very great. Unlike the application of biotechnology to plants, the application of such methods to animals causes far more public concern, much of which is based on ignorance whipped up by the tabloid media. Thus even greater care has to be taken to ensure the wider acceptance of any development in this field.

An excellent example of this is afforded by the opposition to the use of BST (bovine somatotropin) to increase milk yields. Although developed by a genetic procedure this did involve the injection of the BST agent. In fact no evidence has been produced to show that this procedure involved any safety or welfare hazards for either the cattle or the humans who might later eat the meat. According to scaremongers in the media, however, this could be immediately compared to the injection of antibiotics which have been a cause for concern when they entered the food chain. In this case alternative techniques have been developed which do not involve injection of the agent but instead involve using animals which produce it within their own bodies. Interestingly, however, the use of such agents has produced, as with the 'Green Revolution', gains to benefit the better-off farmers most! In the USA, where consumer resistance to using biotechnology-enhanced milk has been severe, a system of intensively managed pasture feeding has been developed instead and found to produce even greater increases in milk yields!

Other biotechnological innovations have, however, been more successful. Sheep with modified genes have been developed that secrete Human Factor IX, the blood-clotting agent required by haemophiliacs, in their milk. Genetically altered sugar beet has been developed which produces insulin needed by diabetics and there are now many examples of genetically altered products being used to prevent serious diseases of farm animals.

As a result of the concerns, both perhaps real and imagined, about the applications of biotechnology, especially to animals, both national governments and the European Union have developed stringent regulations controlling such developments. Whilst the application of biotechnology to the improvement of our traditional food sources of crops and farm animals has had the most immediate impact, there have also been significant developments in more futuristic areas.

Notable amongst these has been the production of synthetic foods from starch and oil waste by growing selected strains of bacteria on these materials. The bacteria form proteins and are then harvested to produce protein-rich food material. Undoubtedly, the idea of eating dried bacteria may be less attractive than a plate of fish and chips or a nice apple! However, in areas of severe food shortage, and especially of protein starvation, the use of such synthetically produced materials as supplements to locally produced plant material could be significant. Tapioca, yams, sago, and breadfruit for example, are all excellent sources of carbohydrate and grow easily in tropical regions where the major problem is shortage of protein foods. The development of such synthetic protein sources could thus make an important contribution to overcoming starvation in many parts of the world.

So far, under the umbrella of biotechnology, we have only examined some methods for making better use of existing agricultural land. However, an alternative is changing the nature of the land. Where suitable land is in short supply, a common approach is to move into previously uncultivated land. Where the technology is available this might involve irrigation or drainage to make previously unavailable areas suitable for farming. Where such sophisticated technology is not available, the most common area to be encroached upon will be forest.

In this case the trees will be removed, including their roots, and this will frequently involve extensive burning. Soil exposed in this way will usually then appear to be in an ideal condition for cultivation. So large areas of food-producing land may be obtained for the loss of a few trees (!), so why should this pose any problems for the environment?

Let's look at this next.

Chapter 3

Living with the Natural World

WHO NEEDS TREES?

Figure 3.1 *'Phew! I could do with some shade!'*

From an aesthetic viewpoint trees are very pleasing to the eye. Many city parks, nature reserves and national parks are wooded or semi-wooded. Although the natural reaction to the above question may be that we all need trees, have you really considered whether they are essential, as opposed to being just nice to have around?

Until Stone Age people began cutting away trees in earnest several thousand years ago, trees were the most widespread form of vegetable life. As our uses for timber have multiplied, trees have become more important to us and, as a result of overuse, many species are now in danger. The British Isles for example were almost completely covered by trees. Today Britain and Ireland have the smallest reserves of any European country with only about 7.5 per cent of the total area now forested. In fact, the percentage of land covered by forest varies greatly throughout the world. Thus, in South America forest accounts for almost 50 per cent of land cover whereas in East Asia this figure is below ten per cent. Over the entire globe the figure for forest cover averages out at around 30 per cent. Bearing in mind what was said earlier about food webs and biomass pyramids, it is immediately obvious that such a large biomass of plant material must have a very significant role to play in maintaining the balance of the biosphere.

Before pursuing this issue further, however, it is important to recognize not only that there are a very large number of different plant species, but that they form a number of very different forest types.

One thing that all trees have in common is that they are all perennial plants, that is, they continue to grow from year to year. In addition, they are all woody rather than herbaceous plants. They usually have a single erect stem or trunk which at a certain height branches out to form a crown (the mass of branches and twigs). The outer surface surrounding the trunk and branches, the bark, is a protective layer of corky tissue. This structure allows the plant, if left undisturbed, to continue growing for many years. Thus some trees may grow to a very great age and so reach massive proportions. Because the rate of wood growth depends greatly on the temperature and water supply, this growth rate will be slower in the winter in temperate zones, or in the dry season in tropical zones. This slower growth produces smaller, more densely packed cells compared to the larger cells produced in the summer or wet season. The result is that a cross section taken across the trunk of a tree shows the familiar rings of darker and lighter coloured wood.

As is well known, counting these rings can give us an accurate measure of the age of a tree. This need not involve cutting the tree down, since measurements can be easily obtained by taking core samples into the trunk. Such methods have shown us that some trees in America may be 4,000 years old! Not surprisingly, trees of such great age are also very large. The world's biggest plants, growing up to heights of over 100 metres, are coast redwood and giant sequoia. Furthermore, the sequoias can have a trunk circumference of up to 30 metres.

These huge plants are representatives of one of the oldest plant families and consist of about 650 species, all of them trees. Nearly all conifers are hardy, evergreen trees with tough, needle-like leaves which make dense, shady forests. Because the leaves are thin and tough, they are not easily damaged by frost and they do not lose much water by evaporation. This enables them to survive very cold, dry climates such as occur especially in the extremes of the northern hemisphere. They are able to use the low amount of sunlight efficiently and therefore grow far more quickly than broad-leaved trees. Thus the sitka spruce will grow at a rate of more than 25 mm a day. Many conifers, for example pine, fir, spruce, cedar, yew, and larch, grow in Britain, particularly in the north, in mountainous areas and on poor soils. Interestingly, the Scots pine is the only indigenous conifer as the others have been introduced from abroad.

When considering the major zones in which land plants are found, ecologists talk of **biomes**. Biome is a general term which describes not only a geographical region, but also the combination of climate, day-length, topography, flora and fauna which give it its unique characteristics. In any given biome, climate is a major influence on the other factors, especially the land-form and the flora, which in turn largely determine the fauna. So it follows that the world's biomes are closely related to the world's climatic zones.

In one of the great biomes of the world, the taiga, the tree component is made up entirely of coniferous trees, most of which are evergreen: the spruces, firs, and pines. In some forests, however, the deciduous larches make up a significant share or even, in some cases, may dominate it.

The next great tree-dominated biome is the temperate forest. This is best considered in two sub-divisions.

Temperate evergreen forests, or Boreal forests, consist largely of various types of pines and firs, and are found mainly in the Western United States, although large areas are also found in Eastern Asia and parts of Western Europe. In the southern hemisphere this type of forest is dominated by some conifers, but also has southern beeches in Chile and New Zealand. In Australia, however, the evergreen temperate forest biome is dominated by eucalyptus. Notice that, in this hemisphere, we are meeting for the first time *broad-leaved* trees.

The other great division of the temperate regions is the deciduous forest. Deciduous forests consist of a much wider range of species of trees growing in moderately humid, continental climates with significant amounts of rainfall in the summer and quite severe winters. Under these conditions broad-leaved trees do well as they have much larger leaves than the conifers, enabling them to photosynthesize quicker and thus get more value out of the summer sun. Because their leaves are so large and soft they cannot stand the cold winters of the temperate regions, and thus nearly all of those living in the cooler parts are deciduous (i.e. they drop their leaves in the winter so that they are not damaged by cold or drought). Nearly all Britain's broadleaves are deciduous, except for a few evergreens such as the holm oak.

Whereas the northern coniferous forests are rather monotonous, with few species of trees and a very limited range of animal life, the temperate deciduous forests, although often still restricted to a few species of trees in any one forest, do support a much wider variety of animals. Such variety makes this type of forest particularly good for investigations by primary school children. Not only is there much scope for identification, sorting, classifying, etc., but in this environment it is quite easy to recognize a variety of food chains and food webs. This work is important to begin to build up the children's understanding of the interrelatedness of living organisms at as early a stage as possible. It is never too soon to learn the dangers of upsetting the delicate balance of natural systems!

The final great tree biome we must consider is the tropical rainforest. We have noted that there are not many species of trees in temperate forests whereas in tropical rainforests there will be hundreds of species. This is also true of the fauna for, whereas an oak wood may support perhaps 100 species of insects, a tropical rainforest would be supporting several thousand different species. Thus anything we learn about the effects of damage to a temperate forest must be multiplied many hundreds of times when considering damage to the tropical rainforest. This is a topic we will return to shortly.

Let us now go on to examine some of the reasons why forests are, and perhaps always have been, under threat from humans.

Few people stop to think how important trees really are to us. The principal raw material obtained from trees is wood. Used as a fuel, wood and coal (the product of trees of earlier geological periods) made possible the smelting of ores and, through the use of metals, the development of all branches of industry. Even today, timber products are one of Britain's largest imports. If timber forests are managed properly, by continually planting trees to replace those felled, then the supply of wood in the forest is virtually inexhaustible. Thus timber can be a renewable resource, but all too often it is used unwisely and not replaced. The conifers spruce, fir and larch provide the wood for the building industry, as it is strong, light, and suitable for making doors, beams, boats, etc. In the furniture industry it is mainly the wood of the broadleaves such as oak, elm, walnut, ash, beech, and certain tropical trees (e.g. mahogany) that is used to make the more decorative pieces. Many of the hardwoods such as beech, oak, birch, maple, and hornbeam are decomposed chemically to give wood alcohol, vinegar, acetone, and pitch oils. The wood of spruce, fir, various pines, and poplar are chemically decomposed to cellulose, which is used in the manufacture of paper, textiles, gun cotton, etc. The proportion of wood processed by chemical means is growing rapidly. Great Britain alone devours seven million tons of paper a year.

Other raw materials which come from trees are oils, resin, and turpentine. These are obtained from live trees by boring holes in the bark and catching the oils in containers placed beneath them. The species used for this purpose are pines, larches, and some subtropical trees. Some of the tropical broadleaved trees yield caoutchouc and latex, which are important in the rubber, textile, and food industries. Tannins obtained from the bark and wood of spruce, ash, chestnut, and false acacia are essential in the leather industry. The medicine quinine, extracted from the bark of the subtropical cinchona tree, has saved many lives and many other important drugs have been derived originally from various tropical rainforest trees. Cork from the cork oak and the amur cork tree, and cotton kapok from the kapok and silk cotton trees are other raw materials of considerable importance.

Look around your environment, or better still, get children doing this, and you will be surprised just how many things that we use in our everyday lives are derived from trees. And, that is before we even mention food! There are many trees that provide us with edible fruits. Lemons, oranges, apples, pears, plums, bananas, figs, dates, walnuts, hazelnuts, chestnuts and almonds – to name but a few! Did you think of all the fruits and leaves that are used to make drinks such as coffee, cocoa, and tea?

So these material benefits might provide an immediate answer to our initial question, 'who needs trees?' But – trees are also extremely useful if left where they are!

Trees and other green plants are the primary producers of the biosphere, converting solar energy into organic compounds which maintain the plants and other living things. Forests fix almost half of the biosphere's total energy. They regulate the microclimate by reducing the dryness of the air, providing shade, lowering the ambient temperature during the day, and reducing the loss of heat during the night. Trees move enormous quantities of water from the soil into the air by the process known as **evapotranspiration**. Water constantly evaporates from small holes called stomata, usually on the underside of leaves, and water continually flows up tubes within the trunk to replace that lost. This water is, in turn, replenished by water drawn from the soil by the roots.

At first sight this might seem a disadvantage to the environment. Surely the trees are causing the soil to dry out? Without this vast input of water vapour *into* the atmosphere, however, an area soon begins to suffer from lack of rainfall and far worse drought ensues. This is because water evaporates too slowly from the soil surface to produce much in the way of rain clouds, yet water is constantly being lost by drainage. The presence of trees reverses this process and makes an area more, not less, fertile. In addition, trees help the soil to retain more moisture, especially after a rainstorm. Without trees the soil is exposed to the full force of heavy rain and much of the valuable topsoil may be washed away. Even if there is little soil loss, only a small proportion of the water falling in infrequent showers will soak into the soil. Most will be lost through run-off. Trees act as buffers which allow water to reach the soil more slowly and so greatly increase the amount which soaks in.

Trees can reduce the noise of traffic, and their leaves help filter the polluted city air. They help to anchor mountainsides and river banks and trap snow, often preventing avalanches.

But, of course, woodlands are not just trees but a collection of thousands of different species (i.e. a habitat) and to remove one species is to upset or kill many or all of the other species. Our use of trees must be planned and controlled if the ecological balance of the biosphere is to be maintained. This is but one aspect of the important topic of conservation, which we will examine next.

Trees and your school

Of course there are many questions that we should ask ourselves about the ways we use our precious tree resources. Some of these issues can be more or less accessible in our teaching.

Let us start with a harder one. Many of our electronic goods such as the computers in our classrooms are made in the Far East. The packing they are boxed in often includes cardboard. In certain cases, the raw material for this cardboard is not sourced from sustainable plantations of timber. It comes from rainforest. This applies to many of the things we purchase. We are all ready to condemn the people that we see in TV images who cut and burn rainforest, but we can be just as guilty albeit in an indirect way.

Packaging is just one example. Another is pet food. Where does the cheap meat come from that we find in pet foods? Not all of it is derived from carcasses in Western Europe! You've guessed it. Those smouldering stumps of great tropical trees have been cleared away to graze cattle – for a while.

In both of these rather obscure cases there *are* things that we can do. The first is to write to manufacturers and question the sources of the products. This in itself helps to promote awareness amongst manufacturers and suppliers. ' ... Aha, so the consumers are concerned. Yes we'd better do something and maybe use this to advertise our products as being environmentally conscious ... '

In technology, we invite children to disassemble artefacts and discuss the functions of various pieces. This can easily be extended to consider not only what materials are made of, but where they might have come from and the consequences of removing them. As is so often the case, teacher-led discussion can play a key role here.

Now a more accessible idea. Tree planting in school grounds is one of the most positive things that children can undertake and in which participation is the key. Many school fields have in the past just been seen as places to play sports and games, yet they are fundamental doorstep environmental resources. Where to plant? Well around the margins is a good place to start. Grassy banks that link surfaces at different levels which are that bit harder to mow are another area. Children can grow trees from seed – preferably native species. Acorns make a superb starting point. Children can 'adopt a tree' and take some responsibility for the wellbeing of their charges – especially watering and weeding back competitors.

Of course you will always be told that trees take too long to grow and children will not see the benefits of their work. This is absolute rubbish. We will all see the benefits of tree planting! In any case there is something to be said for promoting the long-term view in a world dominated by the 'what's in it for me' chase for short-term profits and instant gratification.

A strategy to give you access to almost-instant woodland is to interplant a quick growing species with a slower one. Oak interplanted with willow is a possible pattern. Willow grows very quickly indeed and is cheap to plant. In a managed situation the willow can soon provide the 'feel' of a dense growth and a green canopy overhead, and all the time the oaks are steadily growing. Then one day in the future the willow is cut back and the oaks are there ready to provide their own special dimension to the landscape. Of course, the willow provides an excellent means of hiding the young oak trees – unlike the obvious staked sore thumbs that are planted out ready for vandals to break down again.

Just to convince you a little further about the direct benefits of tree planting in the school grounds consider these points:

- Trees soften the harshness of the made landscape.
- Trees provide habitat diversification and attract a variety of animals to your school grounds and so provide study opportunities.
- Trees provide shade – take a look at the places children will congregate on a hot, sunny day.
- Trees provide shelter. They may reduce storm damage to buildings on wild days – if they are planted far enough away! Also they may reduce heat loss from buildings in wintertime and so promote energy efficiency.
- Trees make a place look inviting. They help promote a 'sense of place.'

There are, of course, children (and some teachers) who would like to see entire playing field surfaces converted to forests – especially on a wet windy games afternoon, but that is another story!

HOW WE THREATEN WILDLIFE

We have seen just how important trees are to maintaining the biosphere. Now we will examine this issue of conservation more broadly.

We are all familiar to some degree with the notion of the natural process of gradual change called **evolution**. As a result of changing conditions, plants and animals that can best adapt to the new conditions survive – survival of the fittest – while those unable to adapt move elsewhere or become extinct.

This process of evolution has resulted in the appearance of an enormous variety of organisms each adapted to a particular ecological niche. Some, like the dinosaurs, have become extinct as they have been replaced by others better adapted to changing conditions. Examples of species which have become extinct in the recent past are the dodo, Steller's sea cow, quagga, Labrador duck, great auk, passenger pigeon, Barbary lion, and Carolina parakeet. Also during the twentieth century the Asiatic cheetah has disappeared from India (although it still exists in Iran) and the grizzly bear has gone from California. At the present time a great many others are nearing extinction. Perhaps the best-known example is the giant panda, which in 1983 had a population of only 1,000 but is now down to 300 and is on the brink of extinction.

Other species are classified as being either rare or, more seriously, endangered. Some of these endangered species now exist in such limited numbers that it is feared they may become extinct unless efforts are made by us to ensure that adequate breeding colonies are established by such species. Examples of endangered species and/or sub-species are the Indian tiger, with perhaps 2,000–3,000 individuals, the Siberian tiger with only 300 left in the wild, and the Bali tiger that may already be extinct, as is the Japan rhinoceros. Although the blue whale, with perhaps less than 6,000, is also considered endangered some nations still insist on hunting this animal. This has occurred despite the efforts of the International Whaling Commission and many voluntary conservation groups to stop this unnecessary slaughter. The polar bear population in the 1950s was down to 5,000 but now appears to have recovered to perhaps as many as 40,000, so is considered a rare, rather than endangered, species. However, if a species becomes rare it is well on the way to becoming endangered and may soon face extinction, therefore all efforts to preserve wildlife must be supported. Once these organisms have been wiped out and are extinct, on the basis of current genetic technology, they can never be replaced.

In the natural world, physical changes may include those to the climate (an extreme example being ice ages) and landforms (including mountain building, continental drift, etc.). As well as these changes in the physical environment, new plants or animals may become established in an area thus changing predator–prey relationships to the detriment of one or more of the original inhabitants.

Since life first appeared on earth, many millions of species of plants and animals have evolved, but one, the human species, has, during the last two million years, occupied vast areas of the Earth's surface. Especially during the last 250 years, the human species has had far-reaching effects on almost all the other organisms that share the Earth.

The evidence of so many species known only by their fossil remains shows that extinction is by no means a new or unusual occurrence in nature. It has been estimated that only one per cent of all the species that have ever inhabited our planet are still alive today. What has changed is that many of the current extinctions are the direct result of our activities, including large-scale deforestation, intensive agriculture, and industrial development which produces atmospheric pollution. What has also changed is the rate of species extinction. A typical estimate of the current rate at which species are becoming extinct is 50,000 species per year, which represents an annual loss of approximately 0.2 to 1 per cent of the world's species. If this estimate is accurate, and the rate of loss is allowed to continue, a very significant proportion of the world's species will have become extinct by 2050.

What we must not forget is that the loss of a species is permanent and apparently irreversible. Building a large dam may destroy habitats so that aquatic species become extinct, but taking down the dam so that the original water flows are recreated will not cause the extinct species to reappear. The increasing interference by humans is accelerating the natural rate of extinctions and thus disturbing the balance of nature. Let us examine some of the reasons for the decline in certain species.

There are two main ways in which plants and animals are destroyed – by deliberate hunting and extermination, and by inadvertent interference with their habitats.

Hunting is a natural process. Carnivores hunt herbivores for food, and man has hunted and fished throughout his history. Undoubtedly, this has led to the extinction of many species. The Lapita people, ancestors of the modern Polynesian race, emigrated from South East Asia to colonize all the great series of islands right across the Pacific Ocean. They reached Fiji, Tonga, and Samoa about 3,000 years ago and, finally, Hawaii about AD 300. During their colonization of the various islands, these people ate fish, turtles, and whatever birds they could catch. The birds, in particular, were easy prey as they had never encountered humans before and, as a result, many species were completely wiped out. In Tonga, for example, of an original population of some 100 species of birds in 1000 BC, only eight remain today. The same story can be uncovered time and again in areas colonized by humans in the distant past. Thus in North America it seems that 73 per cent of the large mammals which existed 1,100 to 1,200 years ago were hunted to extinction by paleo-Indian hunters. Clearly these paleo-Indians, and there were a lot of them, were very skilled big-game hunters!

With the exception of commercial fishing, hunting for food is now largely confined to small groups of people living in remote areas such as the Inuit in North Canada, Pygmies of the Congo Basin, and Australian Aborigines, and these groups rarely hunt their food source to extinction.

Unfortunately some animals are hunted for other reasons, and this has often resulted in the extinction, or near-extinction, of the creatures involved. Some animals are hunted for their skins, for example, alligators and kangaroos. Some, such as seals, polar bears, leopards and foxes, are hunted for their furs. We may destroy animals like rats and mosquitoes because they carry disease, or snakes and tigers because they may be thought dangerous. We try to eradicate animals such as locusts, starlings, or rabbits, that compete with man for food, whilst others, such as foxes in Europe or big game in Africa, may be killed simply for 'sport'.

Plants, too, may be destroyed because they are poisonous. Deadly nightshade is one such example. Some plants are regarded as pests, the so-called 'weeds'. Of course a 'weed' is merely a plant growing in the wrong place, from a human's point of view. Examined from the perspective of biodiversity, however, such plants may be seen as an essential feature of the natural environment. In fact many garden flowers we all now enjoy have been carefully bred from 'weeds'.

In many ways, however, the greatest threats to wildlife are those that are unintentional. Unintentional that is inasmuch as destruction of wildlife is not the primary aim. It is known that some activities will result in damage to our surroundings but we just don't care! The destruction of the environment is seen as just a necessary side effect of no real consequence. Most serious of these is probably the erosion of natural habitats. The clearing of forests or draining of marshes to make room for new housing or to extend farmland are common reasons for such destruction.

Pollution is another serious threat, especially as a result of the over-use of chemical sprays such as insecticides and herbicides or the over-application of chemical fertilizers in farming. We will look more closely at pollution in a later chapter.

Other activities which often lead to the destruction of wildlife include the simplification of ecosystems by replacing a natural habitat with an artificial one. Farming is the most obvious example of this kind of activity. There are other less obvious examples however. One such change in the modern world is the conversion of natural areas to golf courses. This is, for example, becoming a major problem in Malaysia where vast tracts of virgin forest are being bulldozed to make way for golf courses laid down with artificially introduced, foreign grasses. It is not the building of golf courses that is the cause for concern here but the destruction of the forests!

Increase in population results in the growth or urban areas, in the construction of new towns, industrial estates, motorways, and airports, with the resultant loss of countryside and wildlife habitats. Although many species have suffered severely, others have adapted to this change. That is why urban foxes are now a common sight and many motorway verges, cemeteries, sewage plants, and even rubbish dumps have evolved as ecosystems in their own right.

The introduction of new species which compete with existing ones, such as the introduction of rabbits into Australia, mongooses into the West Indies, or grey squirrels into Britain, can have serious and very long-term effects, the outcomes of which cannot be predicted. In Australia the introduction of foreign mammals such as cats, dogs, and rats, as well as rabbits, has resulted in the decimation of the indigenous marsupial populations, many of which have become extinct.

There are some extreme cases of destruction during wartime. The massive shell bombardments of areas during the First World War in Europe resulted in such damage that despite the elapse of more than 80 years since the bombardments, in some areas of Belgium and Northern France the environment has still not recovered fully. But the destruction of the environment has continued. The use of defoliants during the Vietnam conflict was a deliberate act of environmental destruction and, most recently, the release of oil during the Gulf War resulted in massive environmental damage.

The collecting of specimens such wild flowers, eggs, and butterflies can, if indulged in by a large number of people, pose a serious threat to some species. In Great Britain, the Victorians were particularly enthusiastic collectors and the resulting displays were most fashionable. Yet this fashion was responsible for the severe reduction in the numbers of many species. Cases of butterflies and trays of birds' eggs were a familiar sight in many homes, and the professional collectors specialized in the rarer varieties. Plants and insects too suffered at their hands and many species of rare orchid are now threatened with extinction.

With the growth of 'field studies' in education this problem of over-collecting began to pose a more recent problem in many countries. Fortunately, most field centres now ban collecting of any but the most common species and then only allow the collecting of a single specimen for identification. Wherever possible, any collected specimens are returned unharmed to their environment after identification. Another, and more harmful, modern form of collecting is the picking and uprooting of wildflowers in large quantities for planting in domestic gardens. Many which were common enough before the Second World War are now threatened with extinction because of this. The more rare they become, the more valuable they are as collectors' items. The beautiful blue spring gentian has suffered at the hand of greedy gardeners and a similar fate has befallen the drooping saxifrage and the Cheddar pink.

CONSERVATION

Conservation has been around for a long time. As far back as 1870 the first conservation groups were formed in the UK but the movement did not really take off until after the Second World War.

Increasing awareness of the enormous potential we humans have for destroying the environment has led to the development of a significant conservation movement in many countries around the world. Unfortunately, conservation is an overworked word often used with no precise meaning and frequently employed to imply the protection of some special feature or artefact which may be of particular interest to only a few people. However, conservation still remains very much a late twentieth-century concern of the developed world that is able to enjoy the luxury of worrying about the use of resources from a comfortable and secure base. Our generation is probably the first to think seriously about the future of the planet and to seek to conserve it for future generations. In the past, resources were exploited for immediate survival and with little or no thought about the future. If there was any thought about using up resources, it was believed that human ingenuity and adaptability would provide for succeeding generations.

Of course the word conservation includes much more than the maintenance of plants and animals. Conservation of soil, water, air, and mineral resources are all important issues which will be dealt with elsewhere in this book. For the purposes of this section, however, we will concentrate solely on wildlife conservation.

So long as plants and animals are going to be seen as a resource to be used for our benefit, then it is virtually impossible to avoid destroying some forms of life. This inevitably conflicts with the deep-seated belief in our 'stewardship' role on Earth. This idea of reverence for life, that life should not be destroyed needlessly, is found in all cultures. 'Thou shalt not kill' is by no means a uniquely Christian notion and is perhaps most obvious in the Hindu religion. However, what may seem needless killing to some may be regarded as inevitable or even necessary to others. An informed opinion is an essential to establishing a wider view.

The attitude of stewardship can, however, be distorted by anthropomorphism and fanatical support of animal rights. This has little to do with real conservation but can do much harm by association, providing an excuse to those who would dismiss conservation as a preoccupation of a lunatic fringe. As a result, conservation movements can quickly run into opposition, especially when they are seen as simply trying to stop anyone doing anything. No farming, no building, no roads, no anything.

But is this what conservation is really all about? If you look up a dictionary definition of conservation you will probably find something like 'preservation esp. of natural environment' (Oxford English Dictionary). This is really not an adequate definition since 'preservation' implies keeping things as they are, regardless of whether or not their present state is satisfactory.

In attempting to resolve this issue, E. S. Carter ('The Objectives of Conservation', *Biologist*, 39(2), pp. 66–9, 1992) has suggested the following alternative definition of biological conservation: 'the assurance of survival of an existing assemblage of species endemic to or living in a specific habitat or ecosystem'. On this definition, nature conservation involves the maintenance of living, self-reproducing and evolving resources, not necessarily at the current level. In this context 'maintenance' means retaining in being and in good order. Another definition, as used by the Conservation Trust and WFN, is the 'protection and restoration of an environment (perhaps ecosystem would be a better term to use here) by maintaining the natural balance'.

So conservation may go beyond maintenance to include the planned increase of plants or animals of a specific species. This latter definition, by implying that the aim of conservation is to maintain this natural balance, allows for the improvement of the existing situation where necessary. On the other hand, maintaining the natural balance may even occasionally involve the deliberate reduction in numbers of some species to ensure the survival of others. This is always a controversial issue. For example, the culling of African elephants in order to maintain the total environmental balance in some wildlife reserves has caused widespread concern.

Fundamentally, then, conservation is about maintenance. This could be seen to operate in three broad categories:

- Conservation of habitats with no other form of land use as is seen in nature reserves.
- Conservation of habitats in conjunction with other forms of land use such as agriculture and forestry.
- Conservation of habitats which demands changes in agricultural or forestry practices.

Many environments have changed to such an extent as a result of our activities that restoration of a natural balance is impossible, yet in many cases the result may appear to be a 'natural' environment.

Perhaps the classic example of this is seen in the downlands of Southern England. Downland has developed over many years by grazing sheep during the day which were then folded on the stable land at night, so transferring fertility from the grassland to the cropped land. Maintaining these downlands requires grazing with sheep, no imported feed, and keeping soil fertility at low levels. So, in this case, conservation implies the continuation of interference by humans through the application of traditional agricultural practices. However, increasing human populations require more food. These traditional methods operate at low levels of profit so that farmers were under pressure to plough up the downs and plant more profitable monocultures. Fortunately, in Europe, with slowing population growth and efficient agriculture this trend has been reversed and farmers are now paid to leave land fallow and replace meadows and hedges. This situation does not, however, apply to less favoured parts of the world.

Conservation of downlands beautifully illustrates the conflicting interests and Carter (ibid.) suggests a further definition of conservation which clearly illustrates this point: 'the scientific management of natural environments and resources for the purpose of maximising their aesthetic, educational, recreational and economic benefits to society'. Carter's definition is useful as it draws our attention to other aspects of environmental conservation, such as recreation and education, which require examination.

It is a fact that natural habitats are disappearing at an accelerating rate and with them a quarter of the world's biodiversity. An important priority for conservation must be to identify ecosystems which contain a significant range and balance of organisms and to defend these against further encroachment. The Endangered Species Acts of 1973 and 1978 in the United States took a bold step in this direction by protecting under federal law all species of 'fish, wildlife and plants' that are 'endangered and threatened'.

In the previous section we asked the question 'who needs trees?' Perhaps, at this point then, it is reasonable to ask 'who needs wildlife?' It might be easier to answer that question if we had a more complete idea of just how much, and what variety of wildlife there was on the planet! One estimate of the number of species which have been described so far is 1.8 million, with insects, flowering plants, and arthropods other than insects making up over 80 per cent of the total number described. Estimates of the actual number of species on our planet are even more difficult to obtain and range from 5 million to 30 million! Clearly, there is a need to investigate all the unknown species of the world, so that we can gain some idea of the most important ones before they are lost for ever.

We have mentioned biodiversity before, in relation to trees, but now let us look at the broader implications that could arise from loss of biodiversity. Let us start with the most pragmatic, and perhaps utilitarian, of reasons why we should attempt to conserve wildlife: direct economic value.

Direct economic value

A cursory look at the shelves in the local supermarket reveals one of the main benefits of biodiversity, that of providing us with our daily food and drink. Vegetables, fruit, dairy products, fish, meat, tea, coffee, bread, sugar, spices ... the list is almost endless. To these can be added cotton and wool for clothing, leather for footwear, wood for building, gums, dyes, resins, oils, and medicines.

In the 'developed' world, there is far less reliance on wildlife, with the possible exception of fish, to directly supply our food. The animals and plants we cultivate for our food are essentially the ones which were discovered and cultivated by our Neolithic ancestors. The crops and animals chosen were largely determined by where these developments took place, which meant the Mediterranean, Near East, Central Asia, tropical Asia, and Central Southern America. These areas tended to grow a few favoured crops, whereas in other areas, such as North America, quite different crops were used. Had the European settlers of North America followed the feeding habits of the native Americans, the major food crops of the world today might have been very different! Perhaps the world would be as fond of potatoes as the British.

One of the great dangers of relying on a relatively small range of food crops, whether plant or animal, or both, is that some disaster could easily wipe out a major part of our food supply. A classic illustration of this problem arose in Ireland in the late 1840s. A parasitic fungus *Phytophthora infestans* attacked the potato crops causing 'potato blight', and wiped them out for three years. More than a million people died of starvation and hundreds of thousands more emigrated to America to escape the famine. The potatoes grown were virtually all the same variety and there was little other food available. Today, a wide range of genetically different varieties of potatoes are available, so even if such an infestation were to occur again, only some of the crops would be destroyed. However, one can never be complacent, for there is evidence to show that the fungus causing potato blight has evolved new strains which attack the latest varieties of potato! So the need to maintain a wide range of alternative genetic forms is ever present. The custodians of a great variety of potato types are the peasant farmers of the Andes. Small market towns have a delightful variety of potatoes on sale. Yet even here there is a problem. The desire for higher-yielding crops is enticing the farmers away from traditional types and this genetic reservoir is becoming lost to us all.

Another example serves to show how the maintenance of genetic diversity saved the wine industry in Europe from disaster. Towards the end of the nineteenth century, the vineyards of Europe and California (whose vines had been brought from Italy) were attacked by the deadly root louse *Phylloxera*. Fortunately, in the eastern states of America different varieties were grown which proved to be resistant to the infestation. The European varieties of grape vine were able to be grafted onto the resistant American root stocks and so the entire European and Californian wine industry was saved by genetic diversity! Who knows when the genes of some species of wild plant or animal may provide the means to save even more important plants or animals in the future?

So it is clear that biodiversity provides us with an insurance policy against unforeseen circumstances, such as disease or climate change. It is genetic diversity which will provide the variability to enable species to adapt to the new conditions and survive.

The danger of continually inbreeding from a limited genetic stock should not be underestimated. Such inbreeding results in a serious lack of variety so that any changes in the environment cannot be adapted to. Evolution thus cannot work to protect the species as it has done over the previous millions of years. Over 80 per cent of the people in developing countries depend for their health care on traditional medicines made from plant species and, in the previous section, we saw how these natural products are often the starting point for the development of modern drugs by the pharmaceutical industry.

One possibility for developing food supplies for the future may be to make greater use of wild species in farming large areas of the world. It has often been pointed out that many of Africa's game animals fare much better than domestic cattle in the harsh climate, and could be culled for meat. It may, for example, prove better, both ecologically and economically, to farm antelope and zebra in East Africa than to try to introduce or maintain domesticated animals.

Apart from all-out farming, there are various ways in which we can allow limited hunting or harvesting of wild creatures, often combined with some artificial enhancement of their numbers.

Wildlife provides many other economic and practical advantages. For example, greater use could also be made of biological control to combat pests. It is far better to introduce ladybirds to kill aphids than to spray with chemicals. In addition to direct economic benefits, but often linked to them, are the scientific benefits of conserving wildlife. The living world abounds with raw materials for the scientist.

Scientists have learned a great deal about the nature of life and about ecological relationships by studying plants and animals, and much still remains to be discovered. Often scientific research of this kind has directly benefited humankind. Early indications of the effects of pollution can be obtained by studying certain 'indicator' organisms. The 'Green Revolution' led to massive increases in the yields of cereals during the last 30 years by the production of hybrid varieties of rice, wheat, etc. which would not have been possible if there had not been a wide variety of primitive grasses and cereals to provide a gene bank.

Recreation and leisure

Now let us return to the question of using the environment as a source of recreation and leisure activities.

Leisure activities ranging from fishing and bird-watching to the provision of zoos and national parks depend upon the survival of wildlife, and such activities may produce great economic benefits to both developed and developing countries worldwide.

Given the opportunity, it seems that the favoured recreation of a majority of people involves getting out into the 'natural' environment. For many of us there seems to be a psychological benefit from 'going back to nature' and 'getting away from it all', particularly for those of us who live in towns and cities. This may involve visiting wilderness areas such as mountains, moorlands, seashore, or other areas of open countryside. It may involve sports such as fishing or walking, or hobbies such as painting or photography. In many cases the areas visited are more artificially created environments, such as parklands or gardens, but there is still the desire to escape from the constraints of the town environment where so many of us live – even if most visitors never move more than a few metres from their cars!

Other popular recreational activities also involve observation of, if not interaction with, other living things. In North America, where one might expect attendance at sporting events to be the most popular leisure pursuit, you might be surprised to find that visitors flock to zoos, aquaria, and wildlife parks in such vast numbers that they outnumber sports fans. Indeed, some of the most successful, and profitable, amusements in major entertainment complexes, such as 'Seaworld' in Florida, involve observing living things.

There are those who criticize this 'romantic' view of the environment and prefer a more radical approach to environmental conservation, but it cannot be denied that this environmental romanticism is a strong force in many people and one from which conservation has derived significant benefits in the past.

National parks and nature reserves

In England the poet William Wordsworth started the movement which eventually led to the Lake District being designated as a National Park, whilst in the United States, John Muir campaigned for the establishment of the Yosemite National Park and became a founder member of the influential Sierra Club, which was instrumental in persuading President Roosevelt to invoke a massive expansion of the National Parks scheme.

Undoubtedly, tapping this romantic view of the environment as a conservation measure has its dangers. In the English Lake District there is a constant problem posed by the excessive number of visitors to the area and the same is experienced even in much larger parks such as Yosemite in the USA. The problems of maintaining the natural balance of these areas whilst accommodating the desire of vast numbers of people to visit them and experience the pleasures of being in a 'natural' environment are not easily resolved. Even in relatively rich countries such as the UK and the USA, it is not easy to find the money necessary to undertake all the environmental maintenance measures which might be desirable.

In lands such as Africa the problem is far greater, yet so is the need to protect environments which have, up to now, had less interference by humans and which contain many species important to maintaining biological diversity on the Earth. The classic example of this dilemma is found in the game parks in many African countries.

Kenya derives more than one third of its income from tourism, and most of these tourists come to see animals in their natural surroundings in the game parks. Yet the impact of these visitors on the environment may destroy just the 'natural' situation they pay handsomely to see. Vehicles tracking cross-country destroy native plants and, as they crowd around cheetah kills, hyenas and jackals are attracted to the scene and drive the cheetahs away. In an attempt to improve Kenya's wildlife parks, it is hoped to be able to raise about 150 million US dollars to provide better but fewer vehicles, better roads, and more guards and wardens. By these means it is hoped that the tourists will get their money's worth, while the animals are left in greater peace.

There are many other exciting possibilities. In Queensland, the creation of walkways through the forest canopy allows tourists to admire the animals and plants in situ but with minimal disturbance.

Similarly, tourism could be worth a lot more to Brazil and South East Asia than logging and farming, and would do much to save their forests and become a much more permanent source of income. In addition, however, projects originally developed to enhance tourism can also be used to make a very positive contribution to conservation. For example, the North American bison was virtually extinct by 1900, with less than 50 specimens left. 400 years ago there were probably 50 million. Today the population has been built up to two herds of 12,000 in Canada and the USA.

The game parks of Africa are representative of one major class of conservation area, which are often referred to as 'National Parks'. In the United Kingdom, these parks were established in 1949 under the National Parks and Access to the Countryside Act which set up the National Parks Commission. This commission was given the following five important tasks:

- To establish, designate, and manage National Parks.
- To designate areas of Outstanding Natural Beauty.
- To establish long-distance routes for walkers and equestrians.
- To provide information for visitors to countryside areas.
- To publicize a code of conduct for countryside visitors. This was called the Country Code.

If the United States, where the Sierra Club was set up in 1892, the designation of national parks and the establishment of the National Parks Service was aimed very much at preserving 'wilderness' areas, whilst allowing controlled public access. This pattern was similar to that in Canada and parts of Africa rather than the UK. In the UK, national parks such as the Lake District were already heavily populated and farmed, so what was being conserved here was quite different, and legal rights of public access had to be balanced against the rights of existing landowners and tenants. National parks, in some ways, represent the 'middle way' between the demands of conservation and those of recreation.

In nature reserves, the emphasis is more on conservation, and public access tends to be far more controlled, with defined 'nature trails' and large areas with no public access. An important development in recent times has been the designation of marine nature reserves, an ecosystem which had previously been ignored. This has come about largely as a result of the depradations caused by the increasing popularity of diving as a recreation. In some areas the uncontrolled collection of specimens such as coral and the spearing of fish has reduced once thriving ecosystems to underwater deserts.

The problem with many nature reserves is that they are often too small to support adequate populations of all the organisms which make up a viable ecosystem. These populations can be very vulnerable to disturbance, especially if any 'foreign' predators get into the system. That is why they need protection from disturbance. They might be turned into important recreation facilities for 'serious' naturalists, such as bird-watchers. The aim is to avoid them being used for the typical 'family outing' type of recreation.

Countryside parks

Another type of national park is the 'countryside park'. Countryside parks also provide rural recreation areas, but they tend to be more planned with specific recreational facilities for sports such as windsurfing or fishing, and with the provision of picnic sites, car parks, and lavatories. These countryside parks are usually smaller than national parks and have more facilities for people but provide less opportunity for the establishment and maintenance of natural communities.

And zoos of course ...

Perhaps the least-natural form of environment-based recreational areas are places like zoos, botanic gardens, parklands, wildlife parks, and aquaria, in which the conditions are quite artificial and where the problems of maintaining a natural population balance do not arise. Here, public access is not a problem, except for getting enough visitors to make the enterprise economically sound! Increasingly, however, these places have moved away from the 'animals in cages' view to trying to create as 'natural-looking' situations as possible. So in modern zoos it is the visitors who are caged rather than the animals!

Advantages and disadvantages

So what are the advantages and disadvantages of these different forms of environmental recreation?

Let us start with the nature reserves. As we have already seen, the Endangered Species Act of 1973 in the United States was a bold attempt to give some legal force to the protection of endangered species in nature reserves and national parks. Although

Figure 3.2 *'Hey mum – look what this funny human is doing'*

such legal measures are bound to, and in the US certainly have, come into conflict with the interests of landowners, agriculture, and industry, the worldwide extension of this principle will be essential if nature reserves are to survive. At present, it is estimated that only 4.3 per cent of the surface of the Earth enjoys any form of legal protection. This includes many existing nature reserves, national parks, and scientific research stations.

One of the ways to help important species to survive would be to increase this protected area to, perhaps ten per cent. If this is to happen, however, it will be necessary to gain a great deal of public support through education and through allowing access to nature reserves so that people can appreciate the value of preserving them.

This problem is highlighted in the case of the important nature reserve of the Galapagos Islands. The flora and fauna of these islands are important, not only for their historical role in helping Darwin to formulate his evolutionary theory, but for the number of species which still exist there and nowhere else on Earth. Ideally, from the point of view of pure conservation, these islands should be left alone with no immigrant, foreign species on them – and that includes us! But people do live, farm, and fish on the islands and many of the native species have already been lost or are endangered. To combat this situation money is needed, and this can be found from tourism.

So this is the big problem of using the environment for recreation.

Nature reserves, national parks, countryside parks, and wildlife parks all provide a source of change for town dwellers and an opportunity to enjoy the rural environment. These facilities provide the opportunity to educate the broader public about the environment and to gain their support for conservation measures. This education role, always very strong in the activities of the US National Parks Service, has become increasingly appreciated by those responsible for environmental resources in many other parts of the world. This is seen in the increased use of information centres, noticeboards, and guide books in environmental recreation areas.

The economics of maintaining the environment through providing recreational facilities is always difficult. Size is always an advantage as the larger areas can absorb more visitors with less impact on the environment. However, even in huge national parks such as Yosemite or Yellowstone in the US, the massive influx of summer visitors results in roads clogged with a continuous line of cars and 'RVs' – those enormous mobile homes – with resulting noise, pollution, and general disturbance which totally destroys the 'natural' environment the visitors have come for. On the other hand, the income from all these visitors helps to maintain the wilderness areas which most of them never see!

We can now sum up the conflicts between the demands of conservation and the provision of recreational facilities.

Increased car ownership and road improvements intended to relieve congestion have enabled growing town populations to visit countryside which was previously less accessible. Once these areas become accessible the provision of caravan sites, picnic areas, car parks, cafes, shops, and lavatories becomes necessary. It is difficult to make these amenities blend into the background without them detracting from the surrounding scenery, especially if they are not properly maintained.

Footpaths become worn by overuse and worse problems arise if people wander off them in search of less heavily used routes. Damage to walls, fences, and agricultural crops can also result. Coastal footpaths may help reduce the erosion of cliff edges, but if they are not followed, then even greater erosion may occur. As a result, unattractive fences may have to be erected to protect the cliff edges as well as the lives of the walkers. Such accidental damage may be exacerbated by actions such as picking flowers, when rare species of plants may be destroyed. Even common ones can become endangered if this practice is carried too far. Litter seems to be thoughtlessly thrown almost everywhere and pollutes water, poisons domestic animals and wildlife, and reduces the aesthetic value of the countryside. Even the apparently harmless practice of throwing stones into rivers or streams can cause erosion and require extra maintenance by farmers or water bailiffs. Even more serious in some places is deliberate vandalism. This includes the destruction of trees, fences, walls, noticeboards, and almost anything that is easily broken, apparently for 'fun'.

Clearly it is not possible for large numbers of people to enjoy the pleasures of the natural environment which were once enjoyed by only a small proportion of the population without placing additional strains on it.

Whilst recreation can thus be seen to have a role in helping to maintain the wildlife in nature reserves, national parks, and even countryside parks, the conservation role of zoos, botanic gardens and museums designed basically for people to 'gawp' at the animals and plants may seem less obvious.

Let us take the most obvious example first: botanic gardens. The Botanic Gardens at Kew in the UK may be one of the most famous but worldwide there are about 1,300 botanic gardens of many different types. From the technologically advanced 'Climatodrome' of St. Louis, Missouri, to the specialized Arnold Arboretum at Harvard, there are plants which not only provide pleasure to hundreds of thousands of visitors each year, but maintain collections of many of the world's most endangered plant species. Apart from the living plants, many botanic gardens also hold banks of seeds which are carefully maintained in conditions to ensure their viability over many years. Such collections still represent only a tiny fraction of the plants of the Earth but are continually being added to and may be the only way in which some endangered plant species will survive. Once again, it is the income from visitors to many of these botanic gardens which provides much of the income needed to carry on their research and conservation programmes.

Zoos tend to be an altogether more controversial issue than botanic gardens. Undoubtedly, the image of the old-style zoo with distressed animals parading up and down behind bars in bare, concrete cages has caused many people to feel that zoos should be banned altogether and, certainly, many would ask today 'why zoos?' Let us try to answer this question. Only ten or twenty years ago it is probable that zoos saw their role in conservation as largely one of education. By drawing the public's attention to some of the world's most endangered species and by carrying out research into the problems faced by animal species, zoos were seen to play a peripheral role in conservation. However, the realization that the numbers of so many species in the wild were falling below viable breeding numbers prompted some zoos to examine more closely the possibility of maintaining viable breeding stocks of these animals in captivity. With the small numbers held in any one zoo this is very difficult but, if the population of animals held in all the zoos of the world were to be seen as a breeding population, then the chances of success are much greater. For this reason a system of exchanging animals between zoos has been developed and this, coupled with the establishment of detailed computer records of these animals has led to some spectacular breeding successes.

Once populations have been built up again it may then be possible to reintroduce animals to their natural surroundings, so long as these habitats have been restored to a viable state. Such reintroduction programmes depend for their success on the cooperation of the local government and people and, with such support, there have been over 100 which have either been successful or are showing promise.

Alongside these successful breeding and research programmes, modern zoos have made massive strides in their provision for education, and the best of them can offer teachers excellent resources not only for use at the zoo but also to use in the classroom. This material is for use as preparation before a visit as well as to establish what has been learned afterwards.

Museums cannot offer conservation through breeding programmes, but they do carry out much vital research which extends our knowledge of the environment and, like zoos, they offer extensive and very effective educational programmes.

SO WHY BOTHER?

Aside from the obvious practical benefits, we as educators must surely be concerned about the aesthetic benefits of conserving wildlife. The world would be visibly a poorer place without the beauty and variety of wild plants and animals. Imagine what it would be like without trees or birds. Many of our greatest poets and writers have gained inspiration from the beauties of nature.

And finally, what of the moral issue? Surely wildlife has a right to exist? We may regard ourselves as the highest form of living creature but in this case we must therefore have a moral obligation to protect rather than destroy other forms of life. Perhaps the biggest danger to wildlife is lack of *informed* concern. All too often no action is taken, or when it is taken the damage has already been done and cannot be remedied.

Conservation is by no means as simple and straightforward as some would have us believe. Human preferences, by favouring certain species for historical or cultural reasons, or because those species are attractive to humans, may create imbalance. Rates of population growth and the application of new technologies change situations. What may be seen to be acceptable in one part of the world may be impossible to achieve in other areas.

What is clear is that there needs to be a much better understanding of the problems and principles involved if those who make policy decisions, and the larger number who have to make practical decisions on the ground, are to receive the guidance they need. We hope that, from all that has gone before, you will see how essential education is to conservation.

Regulations aimed at minimizing conflict between conservation and recreation can help but it is not only up to planners, but also up to individuals, to see that this valuable but easily destroyed resource is protected yet remains as unmodified as possible. The more we modify the countryside with roads and buildings the less 'natural' and the closer to an extension of the town it becomes. Wild plants and animals can no longer be seen as just objects of amusement for our leisure pursuits, nor as resources to be ruthlessly exploited to extinction. Nor can the environment be seen as something which must be preserved in aspic (or formalin!).

We are part of our environment and we cannot help but interact with it. Foxes, badgers, hedgehogs, many birds and many plants are now as much part of the environment of some towns as they traditionally were of the countryside. We need to learn to share our town environment with these other living things and to appreciate their presence. Education has a vital role in ensuring that our children grow up with sufficient understanding of the environment to enable them to avoid many of the mistakes of the older generation. Nature reserves, national parks, country parks, botanic gardens, zoos, aquaria and museums can also play an important part, but the vital development from mere observation to education will always be down to the teacher.

Wildlife is important, for all the reasons given above, and it is essential that the coming generation are educated to appreciate this. It is also essential that the principles of biodiversity and its conservation are taught in primary and secondary schools as well as colleges and universities. In addition, the natural history museums, zoos and botanic gardens of the world have done much to increase the awareness of the general public about the need to conserve biodiversity and every effort should be made to help them further this work by ensuring that there are adequate resources. It is also essential to encourage the sustainable use of biological resources on a local, national, and international scale. Examples of how this might be achieved at a local level include improving livestock management to minimize pollution from wastes, managing forests so that some parts are used for timber production and others for conservation purposes, and managing reservoirs so that freshwater habitats are maintained.

So what can we, as teachers, do about conservation?

Well here are just a few ideas:

- Support organizations like the World Fund for Nature, Royal Society for the Protection of Birds, Royal Society for Nature Conservation, Royal Society for the Prevention of Cruelty to Animals, Friends of the Earth, Greenpeace, the Conservation Society and the Flora and Fauna Preservation Society.
- Create your own nature reserve, perhaps with a nature trail, around the school.
- If possible, leave part of your garden or school grounds untouched, and keep a record of the changes that take place.
- NEVER uproot wild flowers.
- Collect photographs of butterflies, eggs, birds, etc, never actual specimens!
- Avoid buying things made from wild animal products such as real fur coats, pet food made from whale meat, etc.
- Avoid using chemical sprays, etc. on your garden.
- Plant trees.
- Get your school involved in conservation projects run by local or national conservation organizations. In the UK this would be the British Trust for Conservation Volunteers (BTCV).

Chapter 4

Dig It All Up! – or Reforming the Landscape

Take a look out of the window. What do you see?

The chances are that the human-made world will have a predominant influence on your view. The environment is far from natural. If you are reading this book in an urban area then buildings, walls, roads, street lights and possibly overhead cables visibly demonstrate our master – or is it domination? – of the landscape.

It is a sobering thought that all of these expressions of our modern relationship with our surroundings are founded on digging things up! As a consequence of our need for brick/concrete houses and roads, a great deal of landscape alteration has occurred. This alteration occurs not only at the place where the constructions are made but also at the site from where the raw materials were extracted in the first place.

The bulk materials for the construction industry include things like bricks, sand, cement, and gravel. Typically, it is the sedimentary rocks, those formed as their name suggests by sedimentation, that yield constructional materials in a raw or modified form.

SEDIMENTARY ROCKS

Sedimentary rock types are often derived from deposits of sediment associated with the action of ancient seas. This is usually a result of the erosion of existing rocks via river activities or coastal processes which dump their particulate load into an adjacent aquatic basin. If the particles are very fine, they may become clays. Coarser materials may contribute to sandstones and, more rarely, particles of mixed sizes lead to the formation of rocks such as conglomerates. In many areas, sedimentary rocks are available at or just under the surface of the land and their location is a function of both geological processes and changes to the landscape through erosion so that exposures can be made. See the illustration in Figure 4.1.

The depth at which deposition occurs has an influence on particle size. Those rocks formed under deeper water are usually clays, those formed under more shallow water,

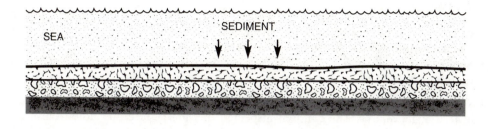

Figure 4.1 *Formation of sedimentary rocks*

such as in deltas, may often produce sandstones and beach deposits with conglomerates.

Not all marine sedimentary rocks are a result of the deposition of particles derived from the breaking down of other rock masses. In the seas of today, just as in the past, other sedimentary processes may be at work. Small creatures may aid the sedimentary process by yielding their skeletal bodies for rock-building. This could be in the form of masses of shells from the bodies of molluscs or brachiopods, or perhaps the successive laying down of coral skeletons as each new generation builds upon the layer beneath.

Some sedimentary rocks of marine, or certainly water-based, origin may be partly due to the precipitation of dissolved substances which have come out of solution. Today there are sediments accumulating by this process around shallow offshoots of the sea in hot, dry climates. Similar processes occur around inland seas and lakes where the water may be characterized by the local in-washing of particular salty compounds, as occurs in some districts along the East African Rift Valley. Here, volcanic activity along the fault lines has brought about the accumulation of a range of alkaline minerals. These are then eroded and washed down into shallow lakes where evaporation may enable them to crystallize. In the USA the famous Salt Lake City is another such site of crystallization.

As we have just hinted, sediments are not just related to processes occurring in the seas. Sedimentation can occur in lake beds, on the seashore, and indeed even in deserts where wind rather than water is the agent of transport and deposition.

From a teaching perspective, sedimentary rocks can be identified because:

• Generally speaking, they are not particularly well consolidated (there are exceptions, especially with older, crystalline lime-containing rocks).

- Sedimentary rocks may show evidence of the process of sedimentation and thus exhibit some evidence of layering. This can be quite pronounced in the case of the laying down of delta sediments or wind-blown particles.
- Sedimentary rocks may contain evidence of the past lives of living things (usually marine) which we know as fossils.

Just a quick teaching anecdote here. Some primary age children were once sent on a visit to a chalk quarry. The children inspected the quarry face and noted the near-horizontal bedding planes and the pattern of joints. They looked at fallen rocks at the base of the quarry face and discovered traces of past life with shapes depicting mollusc shells and sea urchins. On the subsequent de-briefing, the children were asked what a fossil was. One little girl replied without hesitation 'A fossil is an animal that lives in a rock!'

The building industry has a voracious appetite for raw materials derived from sedimentary rocks. Let us have a look at a few of these.

Bulk building materials

Bricks

We will start with clay since this has some importance in terms of our teaching. Much research into teaching and learning has embraced ideas on 'alternative frameworks' – that is taking account of children's understanding and interpretation of the world as they see it. Language can play a fundamental role in the setting up of alternative frameworks.

So now a child's perspective. The word 'rock' to most children will mean something occurring naturally which is hard. We even reinforce this in our everyday speech with phrases like 'as hard as rock'. But not all rocks are hard. A bed of clay, from a geological perspective, is a rock. Exposure to ideas like this may cause 'cognitive conflict' and enable children to set up new mental frameworks to accommodate a science-dedicated, more specific understanding of this term.

Although concrete has had an increasingly high profile in the construction industry, bricks derived from clay have proved to be an enduring building material in the UK. The mellow tones of bricks seem to have a sense of harmony with the landscape that is difficult to achieve with harsh grey concrete. Even dyed or coloured concrete has a cold hard aura. Some buildings have won awards for texturing their concrete with wood-grain patterns. They still look cold and uninviting.

So how are clay bricks made? When they are heated to a sustained high temperature, the tiny particles of which clay is composed begin to undergo changes. What was a damp, plastic substance in the ground now becomes a rigid resistant material which has often changed colour into the bargain!

In the UK, the counties of Oxfordshire, Bedfordshire, and Buckinghamshire have been major brick-producers for many years. One reason for this is that apart from having an abundance of clay, and being situated near to centres of demand like London and Birmingham, the clay has a small, naturally occurring content of oily compounds. This means that the 'firing' of the bricks in kilns is assisted by the bricks themselves and so cuts fuel costs. The consequences of using so much clay to make bricks of course are that there are some awfully big holes left in the ground and there is a considerable amount of fuel used in the firing process. Fuel is also needed to transport the heavy bricks to the building sites. Clusters of tall smoke stacks at brick-making sites still punctuate the landscape of middle England as a testimony to the demand for bricks.

Currently, with the UK in a transition phase into waste recycling, these large holes in the ground are still ideal sites for burying domestic waste. Furthermore, the relative stability of clay as a plastic, impervious rock also makes it ideal as a shock-proof repository for long-term nuclear waste.

In landscape terms, we tend to associate clay with flat lowlands which may have extensive evidence of surface water bodies either as streams or ponds.

Sand and aggregates

Sand and related aggregates are significant across all strands of the construction industry. For example, the building of a typical three-bedroomed house requires 50 tonnes of aggregates. By comparison a ten-storey office block needs around 2,000 tonnes and a mile of motorway needs about 100,000 tonnes! Sand, which can occur as beds in an unconsolidated form, is another example of our contradictory experience of the term 'rock'.

Quarries for sand can yet again leave large holes in the ground. In some cases, sand can be dredged by various means along our coastline rather than come from land-based extraction. This seems like an ideal way of gaining a valuable resource with the minimum of disruption – after all, the sea is a perfect cover-up. It is not quite so simple, because if shallow, sandy banks are destroyed, so too are the fish stocks that inhabit these underwater regions.

Gravel and sands can also be taken from sites adjacent to major rivers where significant deposits may occur. Both the river systems associated with the Trent and the Thames are worked extensively for aggregates. An environmental benefit from this may be the creation of extensive shallow lakes referred to as 'gravel pits' which serve to diversify aquatic and bird life. Gravel pits in the Thames Valley area of the UK have an important leisure application with sailing, fishing, and windsurfing among the activities pursued.

Another source of sand may be from deposits of glacial origin. Sand and gravel can sometimes accumulate as meltwater-charged deltas at the edges of ice sheets and even through wind-blown mechanisms.

The glass-making industry takes advantage of very pure sand deposits, and it will be interesting to see to what extent glass recycling will slow down the demand for quarried sources.

Cement

Lime-bearing rocks, or limestones, are quarried in enormous quantities for use by all developed societies. Harder limestones are prized as road-making aggregates but this can be achieved with many other rocks as well. Softer limestone rocks like chalk have been used in large quantities by farmers for centuries to lime soils, especially heavy clays.

The most important role for limestone rocks today is their central part in the making of cement. Not that making cement is a particularly modern technology! The Romans were expert cement makers and that is why so many of their buildings have survived, at least in part, to this day. They used burnt lime and sand mixed with volcanic ash to make their cement. Modern cement is made in a similar fashion using mainly limestone, clay, and sand. Cement production is the third largest consumer of solid fuel in the UK after domestic consumption including power stations, and iron and steel production.

Generally speaking the softer limestones are most highly-prized simply because they are easier to dig up in the first place. Of soft limestones, chalk, a distinctive white rock, is perhaps one of the more noteworthy.

Chalk landscapes

Chalk is found across great stretches of Europe from France through southern England and then into Scandinavia. The holes created by the digging of chalk in particular have been used in the past for backfilling by domestic rubbish. This is not without problems. Domestic rubbish tips are noted for their production of inflammable gases such as methane from the rotting organic components. This is often flared off from specially constructed pipe networks which collect the gas. Chalk is a rock that is characterized by planes of weakness and sometimes methane leaks out of chalk pit rubbish dumps along these cracks. Indeed the gas can migrate considerable distances and then accumulate in whatever low-lying receptacles it encounters. Sometimes this includes the voids beneath nearby houses. In these circumstances, when an appropriate air–methane mixture is reached and a source of ignition supplied (this could be an electrical spark from a switch), the house duly explodes!

In landscape terms, chalk is noted for the way in which it has been gently folded and eroded to produce steep scarp slopes and gentle back or 'dip' slopes which we recognize as 'downland', and which are illustrated in Figure 4.2.

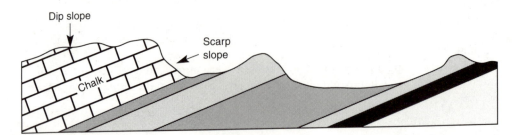

Figure 4.2 *Strata contributing to 'downland' landscape*

As a teaching point, there is an apparent contradiction in many chalk landscapes. Much chalk downland is characterized by an absence of surface drainage. Rainfall quickly passes through the porous rock and accumulates at depth. At the margins of chalk masses, naturally occurring springs may release this water, typically at interfaces with impervious strata such as clay. Yet the classic landforms of chalk downland often include quite spectacular 'dry' valleys. These can be traced through the landscape and frequently they exhibit a dendritic pattern as small contributing valleys join their cousins. Valleys are formed by fluvial activities – running water – so how did dry valleys come about?

The answer may be connected with evidence of past climatic change. Active erosion is not taking place at the valley floor. The valleys we see today are, in a way, representing a sort of 'fossil landscape'. In the past it would seem that southern England had significantly greater amounts of rainfall and small streams and rivers actively flowed through these valleys as a consequence of higher levels of saturated chalk rock beneath.

This in itself is a pointer to some of the more subtle effects of climate change. If, for example as a consequence of global warming, there is higher incidence of rainfall in the UK, then some of our chalkland dry valleys would begin to express this with streams snaking their way through the landscape. Fine in country districts, but not so good when the dry valley has been built on and is now a piece of the urban landscape! Another hidden side effect of raised water tables is that tall buildings which have their foundations in, say, dry chalk would be subject to problems for which there was no design provision if wetter conditions were to become the norm.

In antiquity, chalk downland was characterized by great swathes of beech forest which represented the best-fit or 'climax' vegetation for this sort of terrain in temperate climatic conditions.

Incidentally, it is worth talking with children about how different landscapes have been formed. Many children hold alternative frameworks on agents involved in landscape processes and the leading contender is usually human!

Stand some primary age children on an urban valley margin and get them to look down. Ask them what made the land go down. 'It was dug out so we could put the roads and houses there.' So where has the earth all gone? 'That's what makes the hills.'

Even more telling are the explanations that some children put forward for the directions in which rivers flow. 'Rivers flow from the sea to the land. You can tell that because there is a lot of sea and you see the tide coming in. And the water goes up the rivers and sinks down in marshes and goes down holes in springs back into the Earth.'

Teaching the water cycle as a diagram on the blackboard may not sufficiently challenge the alternative frameworks to which children will tenaciously cling. There is a real need for firsthand experience and for teacher-led discussion that probes and challenges the alternative belief systems of children.

If the children in your class are familiar with the Winnie the Pooh stories, and you have access to a stream, then why not play pooh sticks to find out which way the stream is flowing? With a compass, a map, and a bit of imagination you can soon help them to work out that the stream flows towards, not away from, the sea.

As we have suggested there are a range of rock types that can be used as aggregates. Sometimes as a consequence of removing rocks, whole pieces of landscape – such as hills – can disappear. With some of the limestones, this can have an effect on the capacity of the rock mass to store water. It may lead to a lowering of the level at which the rock is saturated and a drying-up of local springs and bore holes for water supply.

Granites

Apart from hard limestones, other rocks favoured for aggregates include granites. These rocks were formed from the cooling down of intrusions of molten rock. These were usually intruded at depth and have been subsequently revealed by erosion. Granite masses are actively exploited in the West Country and English Midlands. The chippings are exceedingly hardwearing. In passing, it is worth noting one of the peculiarities of Cornish granite masses which have distinctive radioactive properties due to escapes of a gas called radon.

Whilst many granites have some radioactive components, that of Cornish granite is of significant strength. It is especially important since uncontrolled seepages and accumulations of the radioactive gas radon within Cornish granite can present a health risk to the local population.

Media attention so often serves to focus our thoughts on the dangers posed by the disposal of nuclear waste from atomic power stations, and perhaps from medical activities. This may happen to the extent that we may be inclined to forget that radioactive risks are not just the consequence of human activity. Cornish granite is an entirely natural product and the health threat it may pose is real. The National Radiological Protection Board offers very specific advice on minimizing risks and these relate to such things as designing buildings in which radon accumulations cannot occur.

Yet again in connection with West Country granite we need to mention the role of some weathered masses which provide us with the substance *china clay*. One of the minerals which help define granite, feldspar, can in certain circumstances change its character. Instead of being a hard, whitish crystal, it becomes a soft clay substance. It is the basis of much of our ceramics industry and can be found in items ranging from teacups to bathroom sanitaryware.

Britain is a leading producer of this substance and happily the local rail network is being extended to facilitate the fuel-efficient bulk transport of this commodity.

GOING DEEPER ... A BRIEF HISTORY OF COAL

There is an economic consideration which affects the pursuit of natural materials beneath our feet. More or less it comes down to a simple calculation. If the value of a material in our industrial society is greater than the cost of extracting and processing it then it is a viable source. Typically, low-value high-bulk materials are extracted from the surface of the Earth. As the value of materials increases, and this generally corresponds with a decrease in bulk, then the search for them continues underground. Underground mining as opposed to surface working is very expensive. Coal, once the leading player in the spread of the Industrial Revolution, is a substance that straddles the economic boundary between underground and surface methods of extraction.

Coal is a carbon-rich substance characteristically laid down within cycles of sedimentation. The cycles usually embraced a marine incursion with sands and silts which alternated with a terrestrial/swamp environment in which vegetation from great primeval forests was able to accumulate. Subsequent burial and compaction has bequeathed us a treasure trove of fossil fuel. In a way, fossil fuels like coal are simply stores of the bright sunshine which shone in the prehistoric past at a time when early plants were colonizing the surface of the land.

Our industrial ancestors began to exploit early coal seams where, due to exposures via erosion of the landscape, the coal simply occurred literally under their feet. Underground mining was only undertaken when shovelling away a couple of metres of overburden became too difficult and superficial galleries could exploit the coal beds, or seams, for short distances with simple inclines to bring coal to the surface. Valley sides often provided an excellent means of access to seams that ran horizontally, or near so into mountainsides. Today with great machines it is still possible to strip away perhaps ten metres of overburden and extract modest seams of coal and, of course, do so more cheaply than underground mining methods.

This mode of opencast mining tends to strip bare great areas of our landscape and leave a legacy of spoil heaps and decay. This is most noticeable in upland areas where land values are low and soils are thin. Reinstatement of some sort of natural or productive agricultural landscape can be difficult and costly.

The pursuit of thick seams of high-grade coal underground would appear to be an environmentally less damaging prospect. Modern automated coal cutting machinery is designed to make the most of available seams but there is a price to be paid.

As extraction faces slowly progress along coal seams, so a void is left behind the coal cutting machinery. Great hydraulic roof supports are necessary to prevent collapse. These supports are moved along behind each advance of the cutting head which traverses the coal face. When the supports are advanced towards the coal face after the cutting head has made a fresh traverse, there is nothing left to hold up the roof so it caves in behind them. The collapse continues to work its way upwards over a course of years fracturing all rocks above, including any thinner – and at that point in time non-viable – coal seams. Finally there is subsidence at ground level. Most vegetation is able to handle this but small streams may become a little confused and buildings, their owners and insurers find it a thoroughly horrendous event.

The shift away from coal production in the UK has reduced the impact of this sector of the mining industry considerably.

THE VALUE OF METALS

Sources of metals, or ores as they are called, also may be pursued from the surface or underground. Some parts of the world have vast low-grade ore deposits which are initially available at the surface. In the United States there are huge copper deposits which are worked in ever deepening quarries. This sort of activity is acceptable in, say, semi-arid landscapes of negligible agricultural worth. But a deposit of similar size and grade in a more productive landscape would be deemed impractical. Public outcry as well as the cost of land would be a significant factor.

Mines, environment and human survival

The search for metals can thus take us into the political arena. The views of local people and land values mean very little in societies where democracy is a word with no real use in the language, and corruption is the normal means of conducting business.

From the comfort of our ordered Euro-centric lives and from our brief vacation-inspired forays into the wider world, we may not see much amiss from the windows of our luxury air-conditioned coach and the sweetly oiled mechanism of our holiday resort. Real life however is out there and it is a very hard life indeed. In many societies individual survival on a day-to-day basis is central to existence. It is unrealistic to expect such peoples to consider their actions from the point of view of environmental consequences. To them, considering what will happen tomorrow or next year rather takes a back seat to getting through today.

Consider the case of those dwelling in poverty in say South East Asia or Brazil. Let us be a little more specific and instead of talking about 'them' we shall put ourselves in the picture. Imagine yourself in the position of just such a person.

Several weeks ago you saw an aircraft flying around your area in repetitive sweeps. After an aeromagnetic survey, the prospecting team came in and drilled some test holes to confirm the extent and richness of a mineral deposit. Great news! Beneath the rich tropical vegetation near your 'home' in a shanty town are hidden treasures! There is a prospect of some employment if a local mine is opened. There will be construction work and some logging beforehand to clear the forest. Then there will be the chance of working longer term perhaps underground or on the surface where the ores will be crushed and concentrated. You are hardly going to lead the fight to conserve the forest if you have a family with six starving children to support are you?

For most people there simply is no alternative.

But, of course, you don't live in South East Asia or Brazil, so how can you bring any degree of realism about such ideas into the classroom?

There are some excellent teaching resources available these days which help us to probe the issues concerned with the exploitation of resources in developing countries. The larger aid charities have classroom simulation materials available and some of these are very good indeed. They may be free, or at low cost. Beware however ... in some cases these simulations are so good that children will become emotionally involved and your resolve as a classroom teacher will be tested. But then, this is what good simulations are all about, capturing the imagination and spirit of privileged children by setting them in the position of the majority of the disadvantaged people in the world.

If there is one way of broadening the attitudes of our children to issues of development and sustainable living it really has to be through the living drama, role play, and sheer exhaustion of a well-constructed simulation exercise.

Let's now move on to something closer to home.

IRON ORES – BEDROCK OF INDUSTRY

Iron ores play a central role in maintaining our industrial society. Iron and steel are produced from refining iron ores and the metal thus produced underpins activity in the construction, engineering, and manufacturing sectors of our economy. Go into your kitchen. Take a look at the 'white goods' which are made of pressed steel casings and the knives and forks and kitchen gadgets that support culinary endeavour. Go into any office and look at the steel framed furniture and filing cabinets and computer casings. Outside the office there are buildings under construction with giant steel girders clearly visible. The cars in the street are predominantly steel built. We may like to believe that we live in the hi-tech computer age, but heavy industry based on iron and steel is at the heart of all the built things around us.

In the early days of the Industrial Revolution, iron ores were extracted from superficial deposits in South East England. Charcoal from the abundant forests was used to smelt the ore. Streams provided water power to move furnace bellows and lift giant hammers which beat the hot iron into desired shapes.

Little remains of this first small-scale working or iron ore, apart from place name evidence which embraces 'hammer' and 'furnace', and some 'hammer ponds' in counties such as Kent and Sussex.

Later, when coal began to play a role in the smelting process, the 'ironfields' of Northamptonshire made a major contribution to the need for iron ore. The ores were obtained by stripping away the surface and digging out iron-rich sedimentary deposits. Today all you can see in Northamptonshire is fields. The restoration of the landscape has been a success story. UK-produced ores gradually became less and less competitive when high-grade deposits overseas were exploited. In the far north of Scandinavia, for example, huge outcrops of iron-bearing rock could be mined on a massive scale in areas where few people would claim such activity to have severe environmental impact.

A look at the following pie chart, in Figure 4.3, shows that iron, after aluminium, is the second most abundant metal in the Earth's crust. It would seem, therefore, that there should be lots of aluminium mines everywhere to exploit this widespread substance. This is not the case though, since aluminium is difficult to extract from many of its mineral sources. It is bonded into hard silicate minerals such as feldspar and many others from which extraction is not considered economic. Aluminium tends to be extracted from deposits derived from tropical soils. Here the movement of groundwaters serves to concentrate compounds of this metal.

In the UK there is now very little activity in extracting non-iron (or nonferrous) ores. Wales still has a few sites where gold can be found. Lead mining in Derbyshire has long since gone and the once-great Cornish tin industry sometimes has a mine in operation in response to fluctuating metal prices.

The legacy of such old mining sites is a complex one. In Cornwall parts of the landscape are almost haunted by the gaunt ruins of engine houses, or solitary stone chimneys. These were the places where early steam engines were used to pump out the water which saturated the fractured granite rocks and that made Cornish mining so very costly. Another reminder of mining activity includes little fenced circles and cone-shaped 'hats' that protect the unwary from literally falling down mine shafts. There are so many shafts that backfilling would be a costly business, so they are simply made more safe in the cheapest fashion.

Finally there are the spoil heaps. These are mounds of unwanted rock which interrupt the skyline and upon which very little will grow. Tin was not the only metallic substance mined in Cornwall, for copper, lead, silver, and zinc were also found in the

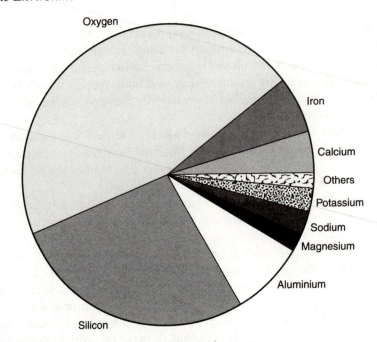

Figure 4.3   *Pie chart to show distribution of elements in the Earth's crust*

veins which traverse the granite. So too was arsenic, a metal-like substance which was disseminated as silvery specks in some parts of the granite. Arsenic has left its own distinctive mark at ancient refining centres. Here it may be present in such quantities in the soil as to inhibit the growth of vegetation.

These examples of problems associated with the underground mining of metals are transferable to many situations across the world. There are physical problems associated with mine buildings, de-watering, and the disposal of rock waste. There are also chemical problems associated with ore refining as we shall see in more detail later.

Let us now look further afield to a mining enterprise in the town of Copper Cliff next to Sudbury, Ontario, Canada. The mines there are concerned with the extraction of the metal nickel, along with some copper and some small quantities of precious metals. The actual ore deposit is believed to have been deposited consequent upon the impact of a meteorite. This crashed into the stable rock mass of the Canadian Shield and caused local intrusions from the melt far down in the core of the Earth. The ores are mined underground and brought to the surface for treatment. They are called 'sulphide ores' because amongst other things the metallic component has been chemically bonded to the element sulphur.

Refining sulphide ores is a process with includes crushing the ore-containing rocks and concentrating the ores themselves. Then the sulphur has to be removed. This is liberated by heating to produce pure ores. A major snag is that a lot of sulphur dioxide is released into the atmosphere. The pollution resulting from this is a problem that we will examine shortly.

As with all environmental issues, there is the question of balance. We have to ask ourselves if the benefits of the use of the material we have gained outweigh the problems of disturbing our surroundings with mining and refining.

YOUR SCHOOL AND ROCKS

Investigations involving rocks and minerals are often undertaken as part of a local study. Further samples can often be collected by children on their holidays. It is often, however, a study of buildings and the materials from which they are made that gives us a direct link between our teaching, rocks, and the environment.

Children should be encouraged to find out what buildings are made from and then to raise questions about the sources of the raw materials. Older buildings will often provide examples of walls constructed from local building stones. They may have clay tiles from locally fired clays or perhaps have roofing materials derived from local stone that splits into thin sheets. The Cotswold area of England has produced limestones that have provided roofing materials and walls for local housing. Slates from North Wales have provided roofing materials that go much further afield and these grey-blue easily split sheets can be seen on older houses in cities all over the UK.

We need to encourage children to ask not only where materials have come from, but also if possible, what were the consequences of their removal. The attitude of curiosity is central to productive investigation. Building materials are an obvious source of inquiry. Less obvious but equally interesting are metallic objects and plastics. These often are processed into forms which look completely unrelated to the source material. Bright colourful plastics are derived principally from oil. The raw material can be dark, in a liquid state of varying viscosity, and have a pungent, sometimes sulphurous smell. Metals as we have seen can have a variety of sources which vary from soft ochre iron ores to glinting crystalline metallic sulphides.

Sorting and classifying materials is a classic piece of investigation which introduces children to ideas on 'man-made' and 'natural' – and requires a great deal of teacher-led discussion to make sense of these ideas!

THROW IT ALL AWAY?

Do children have any idea just how much of the Earth's non-renewable resources are being used up every day? Have they any idea just how much of this material *could* be recycled if we were generally more environmentally aware?

The pie chart below in Figure 4.4 shows the proportions of the different types of recyclable waste we throw away in Britain.

Did you know that, in Britain in the mid-1990s, we use nine million tonnes of paper and cardboard every year but that only about two million tonnes of this is recycled? Furthermore, four-and-a-half million tonnes of this waste comes from domestic households but very little of this is recycled.

Today, most local authorities do provide recycling bins for waste paper but, unfortunately, most of us don't use them! Of even greater concern is that, where much waste paper has been collected, this is not always being used because it is more expensive to recycle this than to make paper from new wood pulp. There is obviously a need for a political decision to reverse this situation.

So how can you interest children in recycling paper? Well, one obvious way is to let them try recycling for themselves. A good place to start is to make a collection of different types of paper and card – new and recycled – and get the children to observe

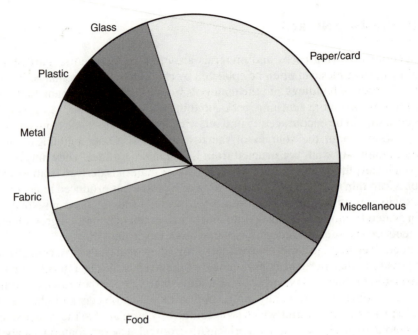

Figure 4.4 *Recyclable waste in British dustbins*

them closely. They will soon find out that one disadvantage of recycled products is that the printing inks from the recycled material makes the products grey. In many cases – for example in egg boxes and cereal boxes – this doesn't matter at all.

There are plenty of recipes available for making recycled paper in the classroom, but essentially all depend on really breaking the paper (newspaper is easiest) down into a pulp in which the fibres are completely separated. A liquidizer is pretty good at this! The pulp is then lifted out onto a fine wire mesh, pressed, and dried to form the recycled product. Organizations such as the Tidy Britain Group have plenty of classroom resources available to help you with recycling projects such as this. The important thing is for children to appreciate both the possibilities and difficulties involved in recycling. For example, if you make them break down the paper by using a hand whisk, they soon learn how much energy has to be put in to make the process work!

What about other recycling projects?

Well you can't recycle glass or plastic in your classroom, but you can compare returnable and non-returnable glass bottles, for example. How do they differ? Which are heavier? How are they packed? Did you know that non-returnable bottles are often sprayed with a material to prevent scratching so they look pristine when bought by the consumer? How could you test this out?

Not only *can* glass be recycled, but old glass is an important component in making new glass and it saves a lot of energy in glass production. On average in Britain we throw away five non-returnable bottles a week – a staggering total of one-and-a-half million tonnes of glass per year, and only about ten per cent of this ends up in bottle banks. What a waste!

Plastics fall into two broad categories, the thermoplastics which can be melted down and the thermosets which can't. OK, so the thermosets can't be recycled, but the thermoplastics can. So why don't we recycle thermoplastics in this country? They do in the Netherlands!

What about metals? The most obvious candidates for recycling are cans. The sort of cans in which baked beans and soup are packaged are made of tin-plated steel and can be easily sorted from other waste by using large electromagnets. Your children can easily test which cans are steel by this simple magnet test.

Drinks cans are often made of aluminium, and this metal is worth considerably more since it is so expensive to produce. In fact it costs ten times as much to produce aluminium from its ore as it does to produce steel. Much of this extra cost is because it requires so much energy for the process. Aluminium cans are thus worth about one penny each, and so are really very worth saving. Yet few places have recycling bins for cans and it is estimated that less than ten per cent of all cans, both steel and aluminium, are recovered. What a waste again!

So what else is in our dustbins which could be recycled? There is usually a fairly small amount of fabric, which could be used in making some high quality paper and various re-constituted cloth materials, such as some mopping-up cloths. The bulk of the rest, as you can see from the pie chart in Figure 4.4, is waste food, and much of this is vegetable matter.

This material can be composted easily to make valuable garden nutrient material. There is much scope for interesting and useful investigations here. Try packing material tightly in an empty plastic container to exclude air and compare the result with material packed less firmly in a container that allows it to breathe. What are the results of making the compost dry or wet? What about insulating the compost in some way? How hot does a good compost heap get?

If you have the space in your school grounds to make some fair-sized compost bins that is great – but you can do a lot with mini-bins made out of plastic and cardboard boxes and frames with plastic garden mesh over them. Animal products should not be used as they encourage vermin and maggots which can pose a health risk. It is best to use only vegetable material in these investigations. And when you've made your compost? Grow some plants in it! Compare growth in sand, ordinary soil, and soil rich in compost. What about chemical fertilizers? They are a lot more expensive than your home-made compost, but are they worth it?

As you can see, there is a lot we can do to get children thinking positively about recycling. Wouldn't it be nice if the children in your class always said 'Don't throw that away – recycle it!'

Chapter 5

All the World's A Dustbin . . . and Everything in it Merely Pollution?

If you were to ask anyone if they approved of pollution it is highly unlikely they would say they did! In the minds of most people pollution is, quite literally a 'dirty word'.

However, when we think back to our Industrial Revolution, where most of our problems with pollution began, we find that people were flocking to the polluted towns because that was where the money was. The expression 'where there's muck there's brass' sums up quite neatly our ambivalent attitude towards pollution. It took a 'smog' in London which killed 4,000 people to generate sufficient concern for the UK government to bring in the Clean Air Act, and it took the River Thames to become so polluted that the stench could be smelt two miles away before controls were brought in to limit the dumping of waste into rivers.

So, although we may all think we know what we, as individuals, mean by pollution, it is not always clear that the same definition will be shared by others. One definition might be that pollution is the accumulation of waste products or waste energy in the environment to such an extent that damage is done to some human interest. Of course, 'damage to a human interest' can be open to a wide range of interpretations and one needs to ask whether a definition based solely on human interest is entirely appropriate.

Perhaps a better way to define pollution might then be 'material or physical processes in the wrong place' – rather like the way we would define 'weeds'. In the right place, and in the right quantity, the 'pollutant' may be not only harmless but beneficial: 'one man's meat is another man's poison'!

The release of radioactivity would generally be a matter of concern and would be considered as pollution. In terms of pollution our world entered a new dimension on 26 April 1986 when the nuclear 'accident' at Chernobyl shocked us into a fresh review of the perils of nuclear energy. They all said it could never happen and yet it did! Ironically the Chernobyl incident occurred as a result of a review of safety procedures at the power station and the testing of backup systems. In order to realistically estimate the effectiveness of some systems others were turned off. Things went badly wrong and what started off as a simulation soon ended up as the real thing.

Few would doubt that the outcome of the Chernobyl explosion was pollution on a massive scale. However, when radioactivity is used in the treatment of cancer it is still radioactive isotopes that are often used (cobalt in this case) but it is unlikely to be counted as a pollutant.

Even more difficult is the question of the use of fertilizers and pesticides in our fields. Undoubtedly, the effects of these chemicals upon the size and quality of the crop produced is beneficial, but in the wrong place and in the wrong quantities these chemicals are considered to be serious pollutants.

So what do we mean by something being in the wrong place?

Firstly, the substance or process in that place in a certain quantity may be dangerous to human health, or may eventually move into places in which it will be dangerous. In these cases the polluting element is pretty clear.

Secondly, the pollutant may destroy wildlife. This moves us away from the narrow, human oriented definition and begins to recognize the wider ecological implications.

Thirdly, it may be wrong 'aesthetically' in that it spoils the 'appearance' of the environment in some way. The pollution of the River Thames, mentioned earlier, may certainly have carried some health risks, but the major polluting element perceived by most people was the awful smell! This last point is important since it brings a consideration of things such as dereliction, or even the growth of caravan sites, within the compass of our consideration of pollution.

What is certain is that the problem of pollution is as old as humanity. In a low density primitive society, however, the disposal of waste is a simple matter. It is when the density of population increases, especially in towns, that pollution becomes a major problem. Historically towns have suffered from sewage in the streets, infestation by rats, accumulation of horse manure, endemic cholera, and air pollution from smoking domestic and industrial chimneys, so why has it become such a major issue in more recent societies?

Firstly, the scale of production of pollutants, including those from agriculture, is such that natural systems, such as rivers, oceans, and the air, can no longer cope with the dispersal of our waste products. Secondly, the enormous range of chemicals, including herbicides and pesticides, as well as radioactive wastes from nuclear plants, are so far removed from natural, organic, wastes that natural breakdown systems cannot cope with their complexity. Horse manure can be described as biodegradable. Radioactive strontium 90 with a 'half life' of nearly 30 years certainly is not! Thirdly, since their ill effects cannot be easily predicted, the combined effects of the quantity and complexity of modern wastes could result in the destruction of the biosphere.

This destruction could result from long-term changes in the climate or from toxic materials entering into food chains. In addition, combinations of pollutants are suspected to be the cause of some of the diseases prevalent in industrial societies. There is much evidence to support the idea that the increase in occurrence of asthma in European children is linked to increasing atmospheric pollution resulting from our continued hunger for more roads. This may be due in part to a cocktail of noxious gases and particulate matter. It is easiest to see the danger when it affects the air we breathe, the water we drink, or the plant and animal foods we eat. That is why pollution affecting us in this way is usually the first to be dealt with.

However, one of the first principles of ecology is that everything is related to everything else. As such, while the links between man and wildlife may not always be immediately apparent, they exist, and the web of life is such that the collapse of wildlife would inevitably be accompanied by the collapse of the human species.

In practice then, pollution must be considered as a whole and not the sum of individual parts. Of necessity, the various components of pollution will have to be considered separately, but it is essential you keep these general principles in mind whilst we examine each aspect in more detail.

Let us then try to list at least the more easily identified examples of pollution.

Air pollutants vary from visible particles of grit and dust, through smoke, to non-visible gases: carbon dioxide, sulphur dioxide, carbon monoxide, nitrogen oxides (especially nitrous oxide), and ozone.

Noise pollution is unwanted sound such as aircraft taking off from an airport, your neighbour's hi-fi playing too loud, or the continuous buzz of motorway traffic.

Light pollution is an increasing problem in modern societies where one may find it difficult to avoid street lighting, advertising lighting, and security lights.

Water pollutants include solids that can block the outlets from sewage works and factories, poisons present in industrial and sewage wastes, acid or alkaline wastes, oil, radioactive wastes, organic matter – mainly cellulose from paper industries, although proteins, carbohydrates, antibiotics, etc. are also present and come from domestic sewage – and, last but not least, heat from power station cooling water outlets.

Thermal (heat) pollution arises from many sources because all activities involving energy result in the emission of heat as in the case of the power station mentioned above.

Soil pollutants. The main ones are fertilizers, pesticides, domestic sewage, and organic and inorganic industrial wastes. However, lead from vehicle exhausts can be significant near main roads.

Dereliction includes disused residential or factory sites, land used for refuse tipping, large holes left by the extraction of coal, iron, limestone, clay, etc. and waste material which is dumped, usually in heaps.

We will now examine each of these areas in detail.

AIR POLLUTION

The earliest known record of an attempt to prevent air pollution in England dates back to 1273 when an ordinance was issued prohibiting the use of coal in London as being 'prejudicial to health'. In 1306 a royal proclamation prohibited the use of coal by artificers in their furnaces. By the reign of Elizabeth I (1558), the situation in London was so bad that she is reported to have complained that smoke issuing from breweries in the vicinity of the palace caused her 'grievous annoyance' and towards the end of her reign the use of coal was prohibited in London while Parliament was sitting.

Approximately half a million tonnes of large particles of grit and dust are emitted in the UK each year, and while dust is an inevitable by-product of working the soil, much is also produced from other sources. Of this total, 64 per cent comes from domestic sources, 19 per cent from industry, 14 per cent from transport and 2 per cent from commercial public services. One of the commonest sources of dust and smoke is cement works, yet the technology does exist to all but eliminate this problem. If the stacks from these works were fitted with devices like water sprays and electrostatic depositors then almost all particulate matter could be removed. The only reason why this is not done

Figure 5.1

is the cost – that is the cost to the cement industry. Of course the *real* cost is to our environment and this does not figure in the balance sheet.

Smoke

The most obvious form of particulate matter pollution is, of course, smoke. Depending on the source, smoke can vary in its make-up. Much of the 'smoke' from a wet bonfire is really water vapour. It is not true to say that 'smoke is smoke is smoke'. Compare the smell of smoke from a domestic coal fire with the odour of smoke from a cigarette with the stench of smoke from a diesel lorry and you will soon see what we mean!

Much smoke pollution arises from domestic fires burning coal, where this is still allowed, or from badly maintained industrial furnaces and boilers and, increasingly, from the burning of forests. Until recently another major source of smoke in the UK was the burning of stubble after the grain harvest, but this practice has now been banned. In many other countries, however, this source of pollution still exists.

These particulate pollutants make surfaces dirty but can also block out the rays of the sun and possibly lower surface temperatures. In fact, one estimate suggests that atmospheric pollution blocks out as much as 40 per cent of the sunlight in Chicago! The extent of particulate pollution does vary widely between different places. Thus figures published in 1988 indicated the following comparative levels of particulate pollution for some major cities: London, 77 units; New York City, 121; Bangkok, 741; Delhi 1062 and Beijing, 1307. The figure for London is interesting since, as a result of the Clean Air Act of 1956, most smoke has been eliminated, as can be seen in Figure 5.2.

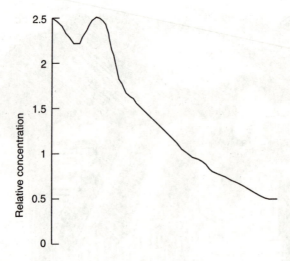

Figure 5.2   *Results of smoke control in London, 1950–1975*

Huge quantities of dust are pumped high into the atmosphere by certain catastrophic volcanic activities. These have been known to affect global weather patterns for years after the event. Unfortunately, of course, we have no control over the forces of nature in this regard, but it should serve as a lesson to us to see what can happen if things get seriously out of hand.

Alongside the elimination of smoke, the Clean Air Act, incidentally, has also led to a major reduction of another serious air pollutant, sulphur dioxide gas. The concentration of sulphur dioxide in the UK fell by over 20 per cent between 1970 and 1984 but, unfortunately, since then it has started to rise again. We will examine this problem later. What is certain is that the successes of the Clean Air Act indicate what can be achieved by the use of sensible legislation, as the following table shows.

Table 5.1   *Death rates attributed to pollution in London 1952–1972*

	Daily concentration in Central London mg/m³		Extra deaths in
Year	Smoke	Sulphur dioxide	Greater London
1952	6,000	3,500	4,000
1962	3,000	3,500	750
1972	200	1,200	Nil

Although the death rate from chronic bronchitis in the UK still compares unfavourably with that in less industrialized parts of the world, it shows a great improvement and demonstrates clearly that the Clean Air Act has saved many lives.

Particles

Unfortunately, the elimination of smoke may not eliminate much more dangerous, but less obvious, forms of airborne pollution, especially a very fine suspension of metal particles. These arise from two major sources, industrial smelting plants and vehicle exhausts.

A couple of examples will suffice to show the dangers of airborne metallic particle pollution. In Poland, in 1985, 27 areas were recognized as so polluted as to be unsafe for people to live in them, yet the inhabitants of these areas made up 30 per cent of the country's population, a total of 11 million people! Clearly moving all these people out was not a viable proposition, although five villages in the area around Glogow were deemed so dangerous that they had to be completely abandoned. The major polluter was a copper smelting plant producing 180,000 tonnes of copper per year and thus of great economic importance. However, this plant also produced 1,700 tonnes of airborne copper particles and the whole surrounding area was contaminated by fine particles of copper, lead, zinc, and cadmium, producing serious crop damage and directly harming the health of the inhabitants.

Since the fall of the Communist system in Poland and other Eastern European countries the extent of pollution arising from such poorly maintained and out-of-date plants has become more widely known. However, even in countries with far more advanced industries the problems can still occur. In Japan it was discovered that people living near a smelting plant were suffering from bone porosity leading to deformation and fractures. The disease, known as Itai-itai, was caused by the heavy metal cadmium. This metal had been thrown out of smelters' chimneys as very fine airborne particles which had settled on rice crops where it had been taken up by the plants. It was from eating this contaminated rice that the inhabitants had contracted the disease. The Japanese government did react quickly to this situation and banned all processes in which cadmium was released.

Around the world there have been many incidents of damage caused by industrial pollution. In Germany, arsenic escaping from the chimneys of a silver works killed rabbits and deer in the surrounding countryside. In the USA and Canada, deer and other mammals have been killed by fluoride gas escapes and in many cases the death of large numbers of birds has been attributed to escapes of various compounds of sulphur.

Lead

In Australia, the New South Wales Health Department reported in 1991 that in Broken Hill, one of Australia's biggest mining communities, more than one in four young children had levels of lead in their blood over the Australian safety limit. Furthermore, a long-term study of almost 500 children living near a smelter at Port Pirie reported in 1992 that lead may permanently impair children's IQ. When the children were three years old, the researchers graded them according to the concentration of lead in their blood. At seven, when their IQ was measured, a five per cent difference in IQ was found between those children who at three years old had 300 micrograms of lead per litre of blood and those with 100 micrograms per litre. Such cases cause justifiable concern and frequently make headlines in the media but, in global terms, they are far less important than a more common source of atmospheric pollution – the motor vehicle.

Peter Baghurst of the University of Adelaide, who reported the Port Pirie findings, has suggested that many thousands of children in industrialized and urban areas may be suffering intellectual impairment as a result of exposure to lead pollution.

Ten years ago it was estimated that 75–85 per cent of the pollutants in the atmosphere above Los Angeles came from motor vehicle exhausts and one of the most damaging of these pollutants was particulate lead. Lead compounds are added to petrol as anti-knock agents. They improve the combustion of the fuel so that it burns smoothly rather than ending in a short explosion. This allows engines to operate at higher pressures giving improved performance and lower fuel consumption. Not only that, but the thin film of lead deposited on the surfaces of the engine acts as a lubricant and reduces wear. However, it has been known for a long time that lead causes behavioural disorders and brain damage in children as well as 'lead encephalitis' in adults which leads to headache, depression, and fatigue. Leaded petrol contains about two grammes per gallon of lead compounds, of which 25–50 per cent becomes airborne when ejected from the exhaust. In 1970 cars in the UK produced 10,000 tonnes of lead compared to only 100 tonnes from the burning of coal products. The larger, heavier particles, amounting to about 56 per cent of the total, settle out within about 100 metres of the road. Analyses of dust in major towns and cities has shown an average content of one per cent lead, rising to five per cent in the most congested urban areas. Still more (22 per cent) is emitted as much smaller, lighter particles which become airborne, much like a gas, and can remain suspended in the air for weeks and may travel long distances.

Eventually, much of this lead will end up being taken up into plants, some of which will be used for food. Thus it has been shown that, since 1946, our intake of lead has increased by ten per cent. As evidence has accumulated to show the dangers of lead pollution, so governments throughout the world have moved to reduce the use of lead, either by differential pricing on petrol, as in the UK, or by legislation, as in the USA. Given that in the UK The Southwood Report (Royal Commission on Environmental Pollution, 9th Report, *Lead in the Environment* HMSO, 1983) recommended that lead in petrol should be completely phased out, progress over much of the world is far too slow for our, or at least our children's, safety. In fact, much of the impetus to reduce lead in petrol arose from concern over another atmospheric pollutant, the nitrogen oxides. To remove these, cars are fitted with catalytic converters but these converters are destroyed by leaded petrol. So attempting to remove one pollutant has been instrumental in removing another!

The quantity of human-created particulate matter is very small compared to the amount of dust thrown up by volcanic eruptions. These can have effects on global temperatures for several years. However, it is the *nature* of the materials we are releasing into the atmosphere which may cause it to have much more serious and long-term effects.

Gases

The main components of gaseous pollution are carbon dioxide, less concentrated but more toxic carbon monoxide, sulphur dioxide, and oxides of nitrogen.

Carbon dioxide will be dealt with at length in the section on global warming. Whilst it is not directly harmful to us, and is essential for green plants, the side effects of its production make it one of the most serious environmental pollutants we know.

Sulphur dioxide, mentioned earlier, is produced by the burning of fossil fuels and in smelting processes, such as the production of nickel. In the UK alone, four to five million tonnes of sulphur dioxide are exhausted into the air each year. In the classic case of the nickel smelter in Sudbury in Canada, mentioned earlier, so much sulphur dioxide was produced that all the vegetation was killed for many kilometres around the plant and the effects could be seen up to 60 kilometres away. Sulphur dioxide not only damages plants by entering them as a gas but, when dissolved in rain, it forms sulphuric acid which enters the streams and rivers making them very acid. High acidities with pHs as low as 4.0 have been recorded, at which levels all life in the water is extinguished. Just to add to the problem, the Sudbury smelter also produced large amounts of fine-particled nickel dust! In response to the local and national outcry, the corporations owning this plant built a 387-metre 'superstack' high chimney which certainly dispersed the pollutants better – but it just gave them in a more dilute form to a lot more people!

Similar attempts to disperse pollutants by building taller chimneys have been used in the UK and the Ruhr with the same results as in Canada. Tall chimneys are not the answer.

Carbon monoxide is a highly lethal gas produced in motor vehicle exhausts and by poorly adjusted gas burners. In fact, any fossil fuel which burns in a restricted oxygen supply will produce carbon monoxide. The all-too-frequent cases of people dying because of fumes from incorrectly adjusted gas appliances are the result of carbon monoxide poisoning, as is the occasional suicide using car exhaust fumes. Carbon monoxide, unlike the nitrogen oxides, is not removed by catalytic converters.

Nitrogen oxides yet again are produced by burning fossil fuels and much of this comes from motor vehicle exhausts. This material will also be dealt with in more detail in the section on global warming and ozone depletion.

In general, as we have seen, locally produced dust, unlike that thrown up by volcanic explosions does not travel very far. Certainly air pollution will naturally be far worse in certain localities, especially in towns. However, the other atmospheric pollutants, fine particles in suspension and gases, disperse far more readily and, since the air circulates freely around the globe, air pollution must be considered as a world problem.

WATER POLLUTION

The next area of pollution to impinge most directly on our lives concerns water. Bodies of inland water and even oceans are largely self cleansing if given sufficient time, but we are pouring material into the rivers and seas at such a rate that this natural mechanism cannot keep up. Water pollution, like the pollution of other media, is a complex problem. The sources of water pollution are numerous, e.g. industrial effluents discharged with limited or zero treatment, effluent from sewage works, and chemicals washed into the waterways by rainfall. Some aspects of water pollution cannot be separated from air pollution since the pollutants arrive in water as a result of being washed down by rain. For example, sulphur dioxide and the oxides of nitrogen end up in water as sulphuric and nitric acids, a topic which is covered more fully in the section on acid rain. The washing of metal particles into streams and rivers might seem less of a hazard as we do not normally think of metals as water soluble. However, small amounts of these metals do dissolve in water and are then readily taken up by plants and animals, including ourselves.

Figure 5.3

Lead

Perhaps the best known example of the danger of dissolved heavy metals is lead. Lead dissolved from lead piping, especially in 'soft' water areas, is now known to present a serious health hazard, leading to just the same symptoms as were mentioned with regard to the intake of lead particles from motor vehicle exhausts. In spite of efforts to remove lead supply pipes and replace them with plastic, in the UK in 1975, ten per cent of households – a total of nearly two million people – still had drinking water which exceeded the EC limits for lead content. Lead poisoning is certainly not a problem new to human society. Studies on the bones of ancient Romans have shown them to contain large amounts of lead and it is suggested that the insanity of emperors such as Caligula resulted from lead poisoning. The Romans not only used lead to convey and store water, but many of the implements they used for eating and drinking were also made from this metal.

As with other forms of pollution, it is not only humans that suffer. All birds, and water birds are no exceptions, take grit into their gizzard (a pouch in the neck) to aid the mechanical breakup of hard food materials. Where fishermen have carelessly discarded lead shot, used as weights on fishing lines, this metal has been taken up by the birds which have then suffered severe poisoning.

We have already seen the hazards posed to health from airborne lead arising from vehicle exhausts, but this is compounded when it is washed off road surfaces into water courses and ends up in the drinking water of farm animals, wildlife, and ourselves.

Mercury

Other examples of poisoning by heavy metal contamination of water have usually arisen as a result of the dumping of industrial waste into water.

A notorious case is that of the poisoning of large numbers of people in Japan who had eaten fish from Minamata Bay contaminated by mercury. Mercury metal is toxic, but organic mercury compounds are far more so and a chemical plant had been found to be dumping both mercury metal and organic mercury compounds into the sea. Fish had taken in these materials and their metabolism had transformed the mercury into even more deadly organic forms. By the 1980s 300 people had died and 1,500 were disabled by convulsions and blindness caused by the effects of mercury compounds on the nervous system.

Other cases of injury or death caused by the dumping of toxic chemicals with metallic components into water have involved cadmium, nickel, arsenic, and aluminium.

Organic matter

Although chemicals arising from industrial sources, such as these heavy metals, are high profile and cause considerable public concern, far greater long-term damage is caused by less obviously toxic materials. We refer here to organic materials which may be natural, such as the fall of leaves in autumn; or man-made, arising from sewage, industries such as brewing and paper-making, and agriculture. This type of pollution also includes agricultural chemicals such as nitrates, and phosphates, which are active plant nutrient salts.

The principal impact of water pollution on the biotic community is usually the removal of dissolved oxygen available for respiration, so that the water becomes **anaerobic**. This usually occurs either through the breakdown of sewage, farm slurry, and silage, or from excessive dead plant material whose growth has been stimulated by the presence of excess nutrient salts. This plant material is largely algae which can produce a 'bloom' that covers the surface of lakes and reservoirs. The nutrients are often the result of the over-use of fertilizers, which are eventually washed into the rivers, and the use of detergents with phosphate components. Nitrates and phosphates are also common components of effluent from sewage works for a human excretes nine grammes of nitrogen compounds and two grammes of phosphorus compounds per day, which means 9,000 kilograms of nitrogen and 2,000 kilograms of phosphorus compounds for every one million people! The problem is that the bacteria that break down the sewage or dead plant material require large amounts of oxygen and it is their respiration which exhausts the dissolved oxygen. This process, known as **eutrophication**, is caused by the existence of 'too much' food and hence excessive productivity. The resulting lack of oxygen is fatal to fish and other aquatic life.

Nitrates

Nitrates, in particular, not only are responsible for promoting eutrophication, but are a direct health hazard in themselves. The World Health Organization recommends that nitrates in public water supplies should not exceed a concentration of 22.6 parts per million. For preference, only half this concentration should be allowed. Excessive nitrates are regarded as a particular danger to bottle-fed infants, but also pose dangers to the health of adults, and have been linked to intestinal cancers. In the UK, in Suffolk, 41 per cent of wells have been found to contain twice the recommended safe limits of nitrates and in Nigeria, where even higher levels were detected, abnormally high levels of gastric cancer were prevalent.

Bacteria and viruses

River and sea bathing can become risky in the presence of sewage where this is discharged into the water. High concentrations of harmful bacteria and viruses may be present causing diseases such as cholera, dysentery, poliomyelitis, and typhoid. The tourist image of gorgeous sand and clear sea around Bondi Beach in Australia may be slightly tarnished by the knowledge that in the mid-1990s the beach was classified as unsafe for sea bathing on average two days out of five during the summer months! It is now appreciated that these micro-organisms may persist, even in the sea, for long periods.

Apart from these 'normal' causes of contamination, water can become contaminated by faulty or overflowing septic tanks and cesspits, by material leaching out of rubbish tips, and by material washed out from industrial sites. In Kent, in the late 1980s, heavy rain caused sewers to overflow and it took 12 days continuous pumping before the contaminated water was made safe.

Solids

A second important impact on biota is that made by pollutants known as suspended solids. These tend to increase the opacity of water, hence they may shade plants and reduce photosynthesis, or may settle in water damaging both animals and plants that live on the river or lake bed. A major source of this type of pollution is paper mills which may deposit vast amounts of waste wood pulp into rivers and lakes.

There are two types of organic pollutants: oxidizable compounds (which are readily broken down chemically, e.g. proteins, etc.) and non-oxidizable compounds (e.g. solvents, pesticides, etc.). The impact of the first type is similar to the process of eutrophication, whilst the second type may be directly toxic to life because they cannot be broken down and will accumulate in food chains. Substances like oils are also a problem as they may alter the physical properties of water. That is to say that they may form a film on the surface which prevents oxygenation of the water, clogs the respiratory surfaces of animals, or cuts down the amount of light penetration.

Water safety

As far as we are concerned, one of our most important concerns is whether water is safe to drink. Water with high concentrations of suspended solids increases the problems and costs of water treatment by directly blocking and clogging treatment plants, and eutrophic waters create problems of storage and regeneration to drinkable standards.

Although the safety of drinking water is a prime cause for concern, we also use water for recreation. Polluted water which is discoloured, foaming with detergents, or with an unpleasant smell is certainly not aesthetically very pleasing! We like to see clear water with fish and other wildlife in it and these are noticeably absent from polluted water. Water pollution may have more direct effects on our recreation. Fishing is the most popular recreation in the UK and water sports such as sailing and windsurfing have been steadily gaining in popularity for some time. Obviously fishing suffers directly from pollution, but falling off your windsurfer into polluted water can be not only unpleasant but potentially quite hazardous. The dangers arising from sewage in coastal waters have been mentioned already but, in inland waters, there is the additional hazard of Vial's disease. This is carried by rats and enters water via their urine. It may be true that 'where there's muck there's brass', but it is also true that 'where there's muck there's rats'!

Of all the impacts of water pollution on our lives, that on recreational use is the most difficult to measure, assess, and remedy, as many of the criteria are subjective. On the other hand, the impact of pollution on the amenity value of water may mean more to the general public than the presence of dangerous but invisible toxins and, as a result, action may be taken to tackle the problems.

There are many examples we could give of the results of failure to tackle these problems but the example of the destruction of a particularly beautiful lake in Russia, Lake Baikal, should serve as a warning to us all.

Lake Baikal is situated in South East Siberia, near the Mongolian border. It is the world's largest volume of fresh (non-salty) water containing 23,000 cubic kilometres, with an area of 31,500 square kilometres and a depth of up to 1,940 metres. It is bigger than all the five Great Lakes of North America combined! How, you may ask, could such a huge volume of water become seriously polluted? Around the shores there has been, for many years, a major logging industry. Unfortunately, over the years as many as one-and-a-half million logs have sunk to the bottom and decayed. The bacteria causing this decay have required vast amounts of oxygen, leading to eutrophication. The removal of the trees has caused massive erosion of the surrounding shores and so the sediment put into the lake both directly and from the 336 rivers that drain into it has caused turbidity and clogged the gills of aquatic animals. The pulp and cellulose mills which process the logs had, in 1985 alone, poured 1.2 million tonnes of waste into the lake.

The surrounding industries and towns associated with them have contributed further pollutants. For example, just one river, the Selenga, was found in 1988 to have discharged 500 tonnes of nitrates, derived from industrial effluent and sewage, into the lake. It has been estimated that over 23 years these factories have discharged up to one-and-a-half billion tonnes of industrial waste into the lake! All of this water pollution is in addition to the 204,000 tonnes of air pollutants!

Once pollution reaches such mammoth proportions the problems of restoring the environment become awe-inspiring. Perhaps an appreciation of the potential outcomes may make us more determined to prevent things getting this bad elsewhere.

The ancients used to think the world was made up of four 'elements' – Earth, Air, Fire, and Water. We have looked at Air and Water, so let's now look at 'Earth' – or perhaps, in this case, the pollution of our land.

LAND POLLUTION

Refuse and litter

Figure 5.4

Let us examine this in relation to two types of land pollution. Firstly, the unsightly but relatively less harmful accumulations of rubbish in the form of tips and litter, and secondly, the less obvious but much more dangerous pollution with waste chemicals.

Litter is clearly a social and educational problem, and where this has been tackled through education there have been significant improvements. In the UK in 1973 a project, originally called the Keep Britain Tidy Group was set up at the then Brighton Polytechnic, with some government support. This later became the Tidy Britain Group and has campaigned for over 20 years to increase public consciousness of environmental issues, especially through the prevention of litter and improved waste management.

Education has always played a vital role in this campaign. In 1994, the group commissioned a survey of 12,500 sites in 57 cities which claimed that up to 60 per cent of Britain was covered in litter and dog mess! However, when compared to the results of a survey taken five years earlier the results demonstrated a 13 per cent improvement in the levels of litter recorded. An interesting statistic from this survey was that 40 per cent of the litter recorded was made up of cigarette ends, packets, and wrappers. The evidence of some improvement demonstrates that, although we still have a long way to go, education and raising public awareness of environmental issues are important factors in improving our surroundings.

Although we referred to litter as relatively less harmful, this should not be taken to mean that we should not be concerned about it. In New York City, it has been calculated that dogs leave 20,000 tonnes of faeces and 3.8 million litres of urine on the streets each year, all of which gets flushed into the city's sewers. Add to this various forms of litter, car washings, oil, and salt from snow clearance, and the cocktail entering the sewers and eventually being discharged to the wider environment is not very pleasant.

The problem of road salt is of particular concern in many Northern European countries. In Northern Ireland, for example, the salt content of Lough Neagh has doubled in the past few years entirely as a result of salt washed from treated roads. This is yet another example of pollution which is more or less directly the result of the increased use of motor vehicles.

Of course the litter and dogs' mess we have just described represents the tip of a rubbish iceberg, for the collected municipal waste is growing with the size of cities and a corresponding increase in consumption of goods and services. The average British city dweller now dumps about one kilogram of refuse each day and much of this could be recycled if it were properly sorted at source. Records of domestic refuse from the 'developed' countries (1990) have shown that our dustbins typically contain 30 per cent paper and card, 8 per cent glass, 8 per cent metal, 5 per cent plastics and 4 per cent textiles, the remaining 45 per cent being made up of a whole range of different materials.

We would certainly not advocate children checking this figure by sorting dustbins! However, the Tidy Britain Group has obtained much useful data from schools which have carried out surveys of litter in their locality. Children should not, of course, be allowed to collect the litter, or to touch it other than by poking around with a long stick to see what is underneath.

Much domestic rubbish could be burnt to provide heating or thermally decomposed to provide fuel, and some plants have successfully produced useful 'fertilizer' pellets from the organic material in such waste. However, very few such installations have been built so far and one of the reasons for this is that sorting waste is very expensive.

The UK government has claimed that householders could not be asked to sort their waste. Yet, where such schemes have been put into effect in continental Europe and even in parts of England, the response has been very positive. Perhaps this is fundamentally an educational rather than an economic problem.

Toxic waste

To the 18 million tonnes of domestic refuse dumped in the UK every year must be added the 20 million tonnes dumped by commerce and industry. Although most of this commercial and industrial refuse consists of packaging materials, it also often contains more hazardous items.

The dumping of poisonous wastes is a matter of serious concern. It is largely carried out on private tips and is unregulated in most countries, only recently becoming subject to legislative control in Europe and North America. Where this has been done it is hoped that legislation will improve the situation by ensuring that toxic wastes are properly documented and only dumped on controlled sites with an impermeable base, such as clay. The danger of unregulated tipping lies not only in the exposure of people to the poisonous substances, but more insidiously via possible seepage into underground water sources. Although newer dumps may prevent the problem of seepage of toxins, there exist many old dumps where the problem will persist for many years to come. Even properly controlled tipping only keeps the problem at bay and leaves the final solution to future generations.

Perhaps the worst example is the dumping of hazardous materials in less developed countries which accept this waste for cash payments. These payments may mean a massive increase in the income of a poor country but are still far below the costs of controlled disposal in Europe. For example, Guinea Bissau was offered a sum equal to its entire Gross National Product – $120 million – to accept 15 million tonnes of waste. In another infamous case, Italian waste was temporarily 'stored' at Koko Beach in Nigeria then brought to Britain in the ship Karin B for disposal. Such episodes raise public awareness of the growing trade in hazardous waste, but do not solve the problem.

Agricultural chemicals

As we saw earlier, our increasing world population has brought about the need for more intensive agriculture, while at the same time polluting the soil with our own sewage and industrial wastes. Much soil pollution results from this intensification of agriculture, which now rivals industry in its potential for harm, although this is largely confined to the 'developed' and 'developing' countries of the world. The main soil pollutants are fertilizers, pesticides, domestic sewage, and organic and inorganic industrial wastes.

We have already seen how agricultural chemicals can be washed through into watercourses and thus pose a serious pollution threat. Weedkillers and pesticides are intentionally toxic to plants and insects and although many of these chemicals, especially the pesticides, are insoluble in water even so they may still pose a serious threat to the environment. About 4,000 tonnes of pesticides are added to the soil in Britain each year, damaging and killing numerous plants and animals. Many older pesticides are persistent, that is, they do not degrade easily to more harmless chemicals, and so remain in the soil for several years. Some chemicals have become so widespread that even Antarctic penguins have been found to have DDT in their bodies. Even we are not immune from this toxic build-up.

More selective and less persistent chemicals are used today in more developed countries, but some dangerously persistent ones are still in use in less developed countries – from which we may import our food products. To illustrate the problem we will examine the case of probably the most famous (or infamous) insecticide, DDT. Now DDT has been banned for use in most of the developed world but the factors leading up to this ban are important.

DDT was first used widely in the mid-1940s and its effect upon the reduction of malaria throughout the world was almost instantaneous. Once its devastating effect upon crop pests was realized the quantities used throughout the world increased rapidly and quickly resulted in much higher crop yields. Until 1962 DDT was universally acknowledged as one of the greatest benefits that progress in science and technology had given us.

In fact, long before 1962 the first harmful side effects were becoming apparent. DDT was not selective and killed off the natural predators as well as the pests. Soon, resistant strains of pest began to appear and as these generally breed faster than their predators, once the DDT resistant strains of insects had developed there were no longer enough natural predators to keep them in check. So it was that pest populations rose rapidly again and crop yields correspondingly diminished.

Although insoluble in water, DDT is soluble in fat and so is passed through the food chains to become concentrated in the tissues of the top consumers, including ourselves! One of the results of this which caused the most public outcry was the loss of birds from DDT poisoning, as documented very emotively in the influential book by Rachel Carson *Silent Spring*.

It is unclear what the increasing exposure to low levels of contamination is doing to human populations or the environment, but we need to note that there is no compelling evidence that such accumulations of pesticides or herbicides cause direct harm to humans. Because pesticides such as DDT are persistent, even after the use of DDT was banned, the vast amounts used over 20 years remained in the soil long after the 1960s and continued to harm wildlife. Although the problems with DDT did promote the search for safer pesticides, as we have seen already, many of the compounds now used are still causing environmental damage.

Radioactive Waste

Perhaps the most difficult problems associated with the disposal of waste on land is associated with the disposal of radioactive waste from nuclear reactors.

Major accidents, such as those at Chernobyl or Three Mile Island, alert us all to the potential dangers of nuclear technology. In the Chernobyl incident, although 30 people died immediately as a result of the explosion or severe radiation burns, many more have died since and the impact of the low level radiation which spread over large areas of Europe may never be fully known. The radioactive cloud that passed over Britain for example served to deposit caesium 137 in a pattern very broadly consistent with rainfall distribution. The caesium 137 was in fact deposited by rainfall and the residual radioactive effect left after the heavy showers that fell on North Wales, Cumbria and north-west Scotland was up to 400 times greater than in southern England.

Such accidents, while spectacular and very serious, are also extremely rare but the day-to-day production of hazardous waste by nuclear reactors is another matter entirely. All reactors produce large quantities of radioactive waste, consisting in part of very long-lived isotopes. This waste must be kept out of reach of all living creatures for perhaps thousands of years before it becomes safe to approach. For every year a one gigawatt reactor is operating it produces an amount of radioactive waste which is 70 million times more active than was the original nuclear fuel.

Opinions on what to do about nuclear waste have an enormous range. There are those who assure us that the technology for disposal is fully developed and perfectly safe. Then again there are others who believe the danger of nuclear waste is so great that the technology should not be used at all. Those who support the continuing use of nuclear power technology claim that, after an initial storage period of perhaps 30 years in cooled, stainless steel containers, the radioactive waste may be incorporated into a glassy substance and then stored under cooling water for as long as required, perhaps 1,000 years. Obviously very strict security and monitoring measures would be needed during this period.

We are certainly not going to put our heads above the parapet in this argument! However, it should be noted that the supporters of nuclear technology – the power generation and nuclear fuel processing companies – and those opposed to using it – groups such as Friends of the Earth – both produce masses of educational resources on the subject. It is up to teachers to use this material in a balanced way so as to give their pupils the information to enable them to make up their own minds on the issues involved.

HEAT POLLUTION

Let us now turn to some less obvious examples of pollution and we will start with one which follows from a problem we have already examined: power generation.

In 1974 the American economist Robert Heilbroner wrote:

> One barrier confronts us with all the force of an ultimatum from nature. It is that all industrial production, including, of course, the extraction of resources, requires the use of energy, and that all energy, including that generated from natural processes such as wind, power or solar radiation, is inextricably involved with the emission of heat. (*An Inquiry into the Human Prospect*, W. W. Norton, Ch.2)

You might think that, 20 years on, this problem would have been solved. Not so!

All types of power station convert only about one-third of their energy source into electricity. The rest of the energy is degraded into heat. It is the need to remove this waste heat that necessitates the building of the huge cooling towers that you often see near power stations. These are a real eyesore and are definitely candidates for being labelled pollution!

But what about the heat itself? On a global scale the amount of heat generated is tiny compared with the amount of energy that arrives at the Earth each day from the Sun. This, by the way, is known as the solar constant and is almost equivalent to the heat from one and a half single bar electric fires (1.5kW) falling on every square metre at the equator (of course not all of this energy reaches the Earth's surface). This is equivalent to every man, woman and child on the Earth burning 28 thousand one bar electric fires 24 hours a day! You can see therefore that the harmful effects of this waste heat are likely to be of local rather than global significance.

Although we may tend to think of the effects of heat emissions on the atmosphere, much of the heat from power stations and industry is, in fact, released into water. Thermal pollution in water can have a number of effects. Some of these are beneficial to aquatic creatures, such as some shellfish which grow very successfully near power station outlets. If it is a nuclear power station, however, you would be well advised not to eat the products of this accelerated growth!

Another effect of increased temperature is that gases dissolve less readily in warmer water. This decreased solubility of oxygen will produce the same effect as over-production of algae or bacteria – a type of eutrophication, which may then damage aquatic organisms.

Our next two forms of pollution are particularly associated with towns and, once again, that motor car!

NOISE POLLUTION

Noise is unwanted sound and can be interpreted as a form of air pollution. It is transmitted by pressure waves, normally through the air.

The main source is from road/air traffic and industry. This is a form of pollution whose effects are much harder to quantify. Where this is extreme, as in some industrial situations, then actual physical harm may be caused to workers. In England 100,000 factory workers have had damage caused to their hearing although in these situations, there are now regulations to control this.

Other cases of easily identifiable noise pollution would include the noise of aircraft, especially near airports, or of motor vehicles near motorways. In these cases measures can be taken to reduce the impact of the noise such as fitting double glazing and the erection of noise deflecting barriers. These measures may be paid for by those causing the noise or by grants from government agencies.

For those living in towns and villages which are subject to heavy traffic usage, however, there is rarely any help to be had from official sources. This is also the case when the noise is caused by events such as road repairs, construction sites, or noisy institutions such as pubs or night clubs. Even more difficult are the problems caused by 'noisy neighbours'. Loud hi-fi equipment, loud parties, barking dogs and so on can all cause serious disturbance yet are difficult to deal with.

The problem of noise pollution is compounded by the fact that, except in the case of industrial or commercial pollution, the assessment of noise pollution can be very subjective. The unit of noise measurement is the **decibel** and in many countries there now exists legislation to limit noise above certain decibel levels. Unfortunately, measurement of decibel levels is not the same as measurement of nuisance levels. This is partly because the nuisance value of a noise depends a great deal on the frequency and duration, as well as on the volume of the sound emitted, and partly because we as individuals react very differently to sounds.

What is certain is that noise pollution is a factor of life in modern society and that this can cause serious disruption of lifestyle and even serious illness and stress in some of us. If you live near an airport you are eight times more likely to enter a mental hospital than if you live in a quiet area.

In Britain today 20 per cent of the population are already subjected to noise levels that, according to the Government-sponsored Noise Advisory Council, are unaccept-able. Educating people to appreciate that noise *is* a form of pollution is an important step on the way to solving the problem.

Figure 5.5

Our next type of pollution, light pollution, is one which has only been appreciated relatively recently.

LIGHT POLLUTION

Once again this is largely a problem in towns and much of the pollution arises directly or indirectly from motor vehicles. In terms of direct light pollution the very bright headlights of motor vehicles are an important safety feature, but can cause serious disturbance to those living near roads. Street lighting is, again, important for safety, both for motor vehicles and as a deterrent to crime. The increasing use of security lights which come on when a building is approached are also important in deterring crime, but can cause real disturbance to those who live opposite such lights and may be trying to sleep.

Light pollution also has a number of side effects. The light haze over our cities makes astronomical observations impossible and thus astronomical observatories have been forced to move to more and more remote locations. At a personal level, city dwellers in particular are denied the awe-inspiring beauty of a clear night sky. Many children for example only connect the name Milky Way with chocolate-covered bars!

The pattern of wildlife can also be disturbed by light pollution and result in animals showing disturbed behaviour patterns. Even some plants may be affected and come into bloom at very peculiar times where light pollution is particularly intense.

DERELICTION

Finally we will mention dereliction. The working definition of dereliction used by the government of the UK is 'Land so damaged by industrial or other development that it is incapable of beneficial use without treatment'.

Probably as much as 100,000 hectares of land is derelict in Great Britain, although much of this land is not officially classed as derelict since it is being used for tipping domestic and industrial waste. Although much derelict land will remain untreated for many years to come, there have been some notable exceptions. The development of Garden Festival sites in the UK at Stoke, Liverpool, and Gateshead gives some indication of what can be done to solve this problem, but also shows the huge investment required. A major success has been the reclamation of slag heaps in Wales, where by careful selection of tolerant plant species and use of fertilizers, such heaps have been effectively transformed.

The establishment of a number of highly successful country parks based around water sports centres developed from old gravel pits is another good example. Derelict canals have been restored for recreational purposes and derelict railways turned into footpaths and country parks. Most of these latter developments have been brought about by bands of amateur enthusiasts, sometimes with help from sympathetic local authorities. Much of the work has been aided by the support of teachers and children from local schools, often working under the guidance of the BTCV (British Trust for Conservation Volunteers). There seems little doubt that children who have taken part in these projects will be loath to see the fruits of their labours being damaged by development or vandalism.

Undoubtedly the amount of derelict land reclaimed by special projects is small compared to the total but 'every little helps' and the involvement of children is likely to have more influence on their ideas than simply talking or reading about them.

Waste is a problem which will not go away so long as we produce it, and the more of us there are, the more waste we will produce. We have to appreciate that the world is not a bottomless dustbin and that solutions other than dumping must be urgently sought.

Chapter 6

All We Need is the Air That We Breathe?

When we looked at the importance of trees to our environment, we noted that they had an important role in maintaining the balance between carbon dioxide and oxygen in the atmosphere. Before looking at this more closely, we need to think a bit more about the atmosphere as a whole. Our atmosphere consists primarily of nitrogen, around 80 per cent, with about 20 per cent oxygen. Apart from carbon dioxide a large number of 'trace gases' make up the remainder of the air's composition and prominent among these are methane and water vapour.

We are all aware of the importance of oxygen for us and nearly all other living organisms to breathe. Perhaps we are less aware of another important role of the gases in the atmosphere. They are involved in trapping heat and enabling us to live comfortably on most of the Earth. If you have ever felt the piercing cold of a clear winter night and wondered why you feel warmer on a cloudy winter night, you have experienced the role of water vapour in the atmosphere acting to keep heat in.

Perhaps the best way to understand what is going on here is to start by looking at the very different conditions on our nearest neighbour in space, the Moon. We know quite a lot about the Moon, especially after the various manned lunar expeditions.

Since the Moon and the Earth are about the same distance from the Sun it is no surprise that they receive about the same amount of heat energy from the Sun per unit area. On the Moon, however, the surface temperature during the day can soar to over 100 degrees Celsius. In the same spot at night, however, the temperature will plunge to minus 150 degrees Celsius – a range of 250 degrees! You wouldn't want to camp out there without a good spacesuit!

On the Earth, by contrast, the coldest place is probably the Antarctic, where a temperature of minus 126 degrees Celsius has been recorded, and the hottest was in Libya where the thermometer one day reached 58 degrees Celsius – a maximum range of only 184 degrees between the coldest and hottest places on Earth. In any one place the range will be very much narrower with even the most extreme difference between day and night temperatures, in some deserts, being no more than 40 degrees. In fact, on the Earth as a whole, the average surface temperature is around 15 degrees Celsius. Clearly there are great differences between the Earth and the Moon.

Until the space probes of recent years many people still believed there might be life on our nearest neighbours, Mars and Venus. The orbits of both these planets are sufficiently close to that of Earth to make a viable climate possible, yet we now know that the average temperature on Mars is a freezing minus 23 degrees Celsius and that on Venus a searing plus 485 degrees Celsius! Under these conditions the chances of meeting a Martian or Venusian – even one with green skin and funny ears – seem pretty remote!

So why are the climates of these near planets so different from our own? Why is ours the favoured planet for life to exist?

Moon landings and Mars probes have shown that the Moon has virtually no atmosphere and Mars has a very thin atmosphere with no clouds. So the heat gained from the Sun during the day is rapidly radiated back into space during the night. Venus, on the other hand, does have a dense atmosphere and lots of clouds. In fact it is so cloudy that Venusians – if there were any – would probably be pretty grumpy because they would never see the Sun! A cloudy day on Earth is colder than a sunny one because the clouds reflect away a lot of the Sun's rays, and the same applies to Venus. However, some heat does get through and it is then trapped by the dense atmosphere and the heat just builds up so that, even at night, the part of the planet facing away from the Sun stays terribly hot.

The differences between the temperatures on the Earth, Moon, Mars, and Venus are due to the great differences in the atmospheres of these bodies. The effect of the atmosphere in trapping heat is known as the **greenhouse effect**. The magnitude of this effect depends not only on the density of the atmosphere, but also on the gases which make it up. Gases which absorb a lot of heat are called **greenhouse gases** and planets like Venus with a cocktail of these gases, which include carbon dioxide for example, end up with very high surface temperatures.

So what is this greenhouse effect, and how does it work?
Let's start with a greenhouse like you may use in your garden. Inside on a sunny day it heats up. We would say that the glass 'keeps the heat in'. This is really a clue to the greenhouse effect. It is something that keeps the heat in.

Have you ever been dazzled on a sunny day by the light reflected from panes of glass on a greenhouse as you walk by? If you have you will not be surprised to hear that the amount of radiation that arrives at the soil inside the greenhouse is less than that which arrives at the soil outside! Yet the air inside the greenhouse is warmer than the air outside. This is because what heat does enter the greenhouse is 'trapped' inside. This effect is even more noticeable at night when the temperature inside the greenhouse can be much higher than outside even though there is much less radiation arriving. So we can see that it is the glass of our greenhouse that is making the difference. See the diagram in Figure 6.1.

Is the Earth's atmosphere the key? Is it like the glass of our greenhouse and if so how does it work? Figure 6.2 illustrates what happens.

The laws of physics tell us that any warm object will radiate energy. Cooler objects emit long wavelength, infrared waves, while hotter ones radiate shorter wavelengths. That is why if you heat up an object it will first radiate infrared. If you heat it further it will begin to glow red hot and eventually even white hot if you keep this up long enough.

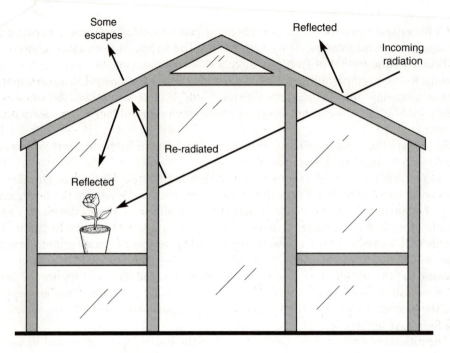

Figure 6.1 *How heat is trapped in a greenhouse*

Our sun, powered by its hot, nuclear fusion reaction, produces radiant energy, much of it in the visible and ultraviolet regions with relatively short wavelengths. Of the sunlight that strikes the Earth, about 70 per cent is absorbed by the planet and its atmosphere, while the other 30 per cent is immediately reflected like the dazzle from

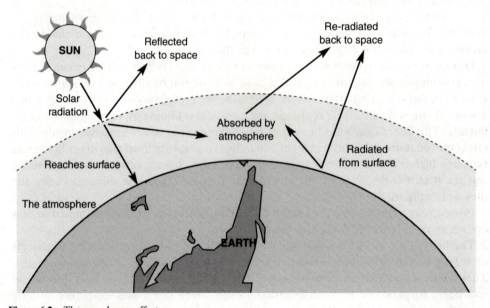

Figure 6.2 *The greenhouse effect*

the greenhouse panes. The heated-up surface of the Earth (much cooler than the Sun of course) now behaves like a bar on an electric fire and re-radiates most of this newly absorbed energy back into space at longer, infrared wavelengths.

Clouds are simply composed of tiny droplets of water. These droplets are formed from the water vapour in the atmosphere. Water vapour and other greenhouse gases keep the Earth warm because their molecules have the ability to absorb some of the infrared radiation being emitted from the Earth. Once warmed, these molecules then radiate a portion of this heat energy back to Earth, creating more warming on the surface of our planet. It is this radiation of infrared energy by the atmospheric gases back to Earth that scientists call the greenhouse effect. As you can see, the existence of greenhouse gases is fundamental to our existence.

So now we can see why the Moon cools down so quickly – the greenhouse effect on it is minimal. On Venus, however, the thick layer of greenhouse gases ensures that much of the radiant energy from the Sun remains trapped beneath. So the surface and the atmosphere get very hot.

So far, we have considered the greenhouse effect as beneficial to us for, without it, the Earth would have extremes of temperature and be a dead body just like the Moon. However, as we have just seen in the case of Venus, too much of a good thing results in the temperature climbing too high. This change in the balance of temperature brought about by the makeup in the atmosphere brings us to the topic of 'global warming'.

GLOBAL WARMING

This is a subject which has possibly caused more acrimonious scientific argument than any other topic this century! The arguments hinge around the question of whether or not the Earth really is getting warmer and the difficulty in interpreting the data which are available. The problem is that those who wish to make a case to support their own views can easily produce spurious arguments.

One of the most 'natural' greenhouse gases on our planet is carbon dioxide. If carbon dioxide levels were to rise in the atmosphere then this would inevitably lead to an increase in the natural greenhouse effect and so to a rise in global temperature.

Antarctic ice may be a useful measure of possible global warming. In the mid-1990s it was discovered that a huge piece of ice containing 500 cubic kilometres of frozen water had broken away from the Antarctic peninsula. Scientists of the British Antarctic Survey believed this suggested that a new climatic pattern was emerging in the Antarctic region. Measurements taken in the Antarctic have shown the average temperature there to have risen more than two degrees Celsius since 1930. Even more significant, however, is the fact that 50 per cent of this warming has taken place in the last 20 years. Ice sheets have taken several centuries to form. Glaciologists with the British Antarctic Survey have pointed out that the disintegration of these ancient sheets has taken place very rapidly in the warming conditions of the last few decades. If there had been a warmer period in the last several centuries, the ice shelves of the Antarctic could not have built up.

So, Antarctic ice *is* melting and global warming is a fact. Is there any other evidence of global warming mechanisms operating? An important point to recognize here is that carbon dioxide is not the only, or by any means the most potent, greenhouse gas.

Methane is another naturally produced gas, being formed by organic decomposition and in the guts of many animals. There are others which have entered the atmosphere in large part, or totally, as a result of our human activities. Oxides of nitrogen are produced naturally in small amounts, but far more is produced by our activities, and the most potent greenhouse gases of all, the chlorofluorocarbons (CFCs), and a number of related chemicals, are synthetic gases produced only by us.

Although carbon dioxide is by far the largest component of the greenhouse gases mentioned earlier, the others are important because of their greater capacity to absorb long infrared radiation from the surface of the Earth, and thus prevent this energy escaping back into space. Compared to carbon dioxide, methane is 30 times more effective as a greenhouse gas. Oxides of nitrogen are 160 times more effective and CFCs are a whopping 17,000!

If we now look at the total contributions of the various gases to global warming we can see that, although small in total amounts, the 'new' components added by us are having a major influence on the total. See Figure 6.3.

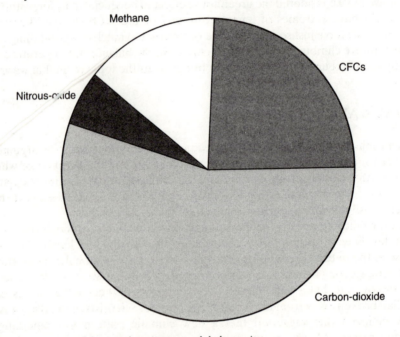

Figure 6.3   *Contributions of the greenhouse gases to global warming*

Before going on to examine each of these gases in more detail, it is important to remember that we have been concentrating on the *enhanced* greenhouse effect (EGE) brought about by human activities, especially since the Industrial Revolution.

These gases are not, however, the most important components of the atmosphere in terms of the 'natural' greenhouse effect. This accolade falls to water vapour. Water vapour accounts for twice as much re-radiation of absorbed energy as does carbon dioxide and so is, by far, the most important greenhouse gas. Not that it is quite that simple! If the Earth does warm up then more water will evaporate. The increased water vapour in the atmosphere would then increase the greenhouse effect leading to further heating, and so on. Thus the increased heating effect caused by any greenhouse gas is going to be multiplied by the increase in water vapour in the atmosphere. Once the delicate balance of heat gain and heat loss is upset, who knows where it will lead?

Let us now go on to examine the other greenhouse gases in more detail, and let's start with the big one, carbon dioxide.

Carbon dioxide

We have already seen how carbon dioxide is produced naturally by the respiration of living organisms so now we will examine the other sources of this gas. The biggest culprit is carbon dioxide gas generated by our burning of fossil fuels and forests. Approximately 80 per cent of atmospheric carbon dioxide increases are due to our use of fossil fuels: oil, coal, and gas. These fossil energy sources first came into use with the burning of coal during the Industrial Revolution in the 1700s but their use has accelerated in the past 100 years, as more convenient oil and gas fuels became popular.

Since 1945 petroleum consumption has increased dramatically, due in large part to increased use of motor vehicles throughout the world, including the substitution of mechanized farm machinery for animal power. When our world population was relatively small, no one worried about what happened to the waste products of combustion – carbon dioxide dispersed into the seemingly limitless atmosphere and was forgotten. Records suggest that the level of carbon dioxide has been increasing by about 0.4 per cent per year from a level of 315 parts per million in 1958 to 353 PPM in 1990. Clearly, Earth's natural mechanisms for absorbing carbon dioxide from the atmosphere cannot handle the large quantities of carbon dioxide being added by modern societies.

About 50 per cent of the carbon dioxide being emitted each year is absorbed by trees and the oceans, much of the latter going to form the calcified shells of sea creatures. The rest remains in the atmosphere. This proportion may, however, be changing.

We have already seen that the loss of carbon-dioxide-absorbing trees is a major concern, but even the capacity of the oceans to absorb carbon dioxide is under threat. Unlike solids, the amount of a gas which can dissolve in water reduces as the temperature of the water rises. So, whilst a hot cup of coffee will dissolve more sugar than a cold one, a cold pond will dissolve more oxygen than a hot one. This is why fish and other pond dwellers may suffer during a very warm spell. Thus, if global warming results in the oceans warming up, even very slightly, their capacity to absorb carbon dioxide will be reduced. This would lead to a cycle in which more carbon dioxide in the atmosphere leads to more warming and less absorption by oceans. Once again we see the run-away effect in operation.

Methane

So how about our other natural gas, methane? Methane is a natural part of the atmosphere and ice core records show how levels of methane rise and fall with global temperature just like carbon dioxide.

Methane, commonly known as 'swamp gas', is formed by bacterial action in wet locations where oxygen is in short supply such as swamps and rubbish tips. The digestive systems of cattle, termites, and even humans all produce methane. If this gas builds up to uncomfortable levels in the digestive systems of cattle, farmers sometimes release it by puncturing the poor animal's gut, but there have been cases of explosions caused by this technique when the farmer was smoking!

Because increased temperature accelerates bacterial activity, small temperature rises can result in large increases in methane production – for example in swamps. So some of the observed 1.0 per cent annual increase in methane is probably due to the current greenhouse heating of the Earth – it is that multiplication effect again! Temperature changes may help explain why we see fluctuations in methane levels in ice cores laid down during glacial and interglacial periods.

Like carbon dioxide, however, methane produced by many of our industrial activities is of increasing importance. Some methane leaks out of the ground when coal is mined. Mainly, though, it is methane as a principal component of natural gas leaking from gas transmission pipes that adds to the atmosphere.

Recent studies have shown methane levels to be very high in most cities in Eastern Europe, where the natural gas distribution system has fallen into such disrepair that an estimated 10 per cent of the gas leaks into the air, never reaching its destination! However, even in the United States, leaks in the gas distribution system are estimated to be at about two per cent and, overall, industrial sources are estimated to account for perhaps 20 per cent of global methane emissions.

Oxides of nitrogen

Levels of these gases are increasing about 0.3 per cent per year but, unlike carbon dioxide or methane, very little of the nitrogen oxides in the atmosphere arises from natural sources. Some are formed in lightning strikes, some in volcanic eruptions, but the vast majority are produced by our activities. Two important sources of oxides of nitrogen, especially nitrous oxide ('laughing gas'), are the decomposition of chemical fertilizers and the burning of forests. When forest land is cleared by burning, large amounts of nitrous oxide are released, but it doesn't stop there. Newly cleared forest soil continues to release large amounts of nitrous oxide even after the initial fire, for the next year or so. Halting the burning of large rainforest areas is one way to slow the increase of this gas, which has an average lifetime in the atmosphere of 150 years. By far the largest amount of nitrous oxide comes from burning fossil fuels such as coal and especially from vehicle exhausts.

CFCs, HCFCs, etc.

Next we come to what are perhaps the greatest villains in the piece – the CFCs, HFCs (hydrofluorocarbons) and HCFCs (hydrochlorofluorocarbons). These are synthetic gases, produced only in chemical factories. CFCs, HFCs and HCFCs are chemically very stable – at least until they get to the upper levels of the atmosphere.

CFC gases have been added to the atmosphere since 1930, when they were first commercially produced for refrigerators. Since then they have also been used for air conditioning, fire extinguishers, aerosols, cleaning solvents (especially in the electronics industry), and as a blowing agent for plastic foams, such as expanded polystyrene cups and food containers. While these gases have been around for only 60 years, they have been added to the atmosphere at such rapid rates that they have become very important greenhouse gases.

Even though they are measured in very low concentrations – 230 parts per trillion for one CFC measured in 1986 – their infrared absorption properties are very strong. Thus a single CFC molecule has the same greenhouse effect as 17,000 molecules of carbon dioxide. In the past few decades, their use has grown rapidly, with measured increase rates in the atmosphere of as high as 12 per cent per year. One report has stated that CFC gases already account for 25 per cent of the greenhouse effect.

WHAT ABOUT OZONE?

Before leaving the topic of greenhouse gases, there is one other gas we must deal with, and that is ozone. Ozone is an allotrope (atoms of an element arranged in an alternative way) of oxygen which contains three atoms in each molecule instead of two as in normal atmospheric oxygen. Ozone is not that 'fresh' smell you get at the seaside! It is, however, that nasty smell you get when your photocopier or other electrical device starts 'arcing', or making electrical sparks.

Ozone is another by-product of fossil fuel combustion but is produced through a set of complex photochemical reactions rather than being produced directly. Because nitrogen oxides are so important for its formation, the largest quantities of ozone are produced where traffic pollution is at its worst. Because this low level, or **tropospheric**, ozone is a strong absorber of infrared radiation it is another, albeit small, contributor to the list of greenhouse gases.

So is the enhanced greenhouse effect a threat?

Whilst one might say the jury is still out on the direct evidence of temperature measurements, there seems to be a lot of indirect evidence to suggest that global warming is a reality during the latter half of our present century. What is of greatest concern, however, is what may happen if the present rate of increase of greenhouse gas input into the atmosphere continues.

Ozone depletion

In dealing with ozone in relation to the environment we must be careful about where the ozone we are talking about is to be found. There has been much discussion of the 'ozone hole' but this refers to ozone much higher up in the atmosphere, in the stratosphere which is 15 to 55 kilometres above the surface of the Earth. It is also important to appreciate that this ozone 'hole' is not really a puncture wound in the atmosphere but rather a region in which the density of ozone is very much less than normal. The ozone layer has therefore become thinned-out in places.

Let us now think about this high level ozone hole. As we have already seen, ozone is a gas – so how can you have a hole in a gas? Where is this gas? How did it get there? Does it matter? These are all very reasonable questions to ask about something which seems so distant as to be of little importance to our lives. As we set out to answer these questions, however, it will soon become clear that the ozone hole may have a far greater impact on our lives than is at first obvious.

Let us start then by establishing what the ozone layer is.

Ozone, you may remember, is a special form of oxygen in which each molecule is made up of three atoms of oxygen instead of the normal two. It is a pale blue gas with a very pungent smell and is highly toxic, so it is a good thing that it is rare in the part of the atmosphere we live in! In fact 90 per cent of the ozone in the atmosphere is in the stratosphere, 20 to 35 kilometres above the surface where it forms the 'ozone layer'. So, how does it get there?

Apart from the normal visible light and the infrared, heat, radiation, the Sun produces a stream of other forms of radiation including X-rays, radio waves, and a lot of ultra-violet radiation. Now ultra-violet radiation comes in a range of wavelengths of varying energies. Ultra-violet radiations are grouped together and labelled UVA, UVB, and UVC. Of these, UVA is the least energetic and UVC the most energetic. As this radiation strikes the stratosphere, the higher energy UVC and UVB are absorbed by ozone molecules which are consequently split apart into single oxygen atoms and oxygen molecules.

These single, very active atoms now attach themselves to molecules of normal oxygen, which you remember have two atoms per molecule, to form molecules of ozone – three atoms per molecule. This mechanism and the ozone it produces absorbs all the UVC and most of the UVB, but lets the UVA through. If you are still unwise enough to sunbathe on the beach during your summer holidays, the browning of your skin is the result of its absorbing the UVA and UVB radiation. It is the energetic UVB which causes the most skin damage and it is this that a good suntan lotion will attempt to block out. The damage by UVB does not, however, stop at sunburn. It is this radiation which is the major cause of skin cancer, although UVA is now known to be implicated as well.

Since ozone in the stratosphere is responsible for removing much of the damaging UVB radiation, any reduction in the amount of ozone would have serious consequences for all life on the Earth, not just ourselves. It has been calculated that a one per cent reduction in the ozone layer would increase the UVB reaching the surface by two per cent and that this, in turn, would lead to a two per cent increase in skin cancer. Not only that, but UVB damages the body's immune system making us more susceptible to a whole range of diseases, damages life in both fresh and salt water environments, and interferes with the efficiency of photosynthesis.

So we need ozone in the stratosphere, but what, and where, is the ozone hole? As to what – well Figure 6.4 is a drawing of the ozone hole!

Maps like this, showing the hole in the ozone, have been produced by satellite measurements of the concentrations of ozone in the stratosphere. These show different concentrations, measured in **Dobson Units**, at different regions, with the lowest in the centre, over the South Pole.

It has been shown that the ozone concentration has been falling over Antarctica for some time. The fall in ozone concentration over the South Pole in the spring of 1987 was so large that the original records received by NASA from satellites were far below the normal and the data was rejected as an error! Rapid further research was undertaken and, later in 1987, NASA produced the results of a two-year study showing reductions in ozone of five per cent. Just remember what we said above about the predicted effects of a one per cent reduction to see the danger!

You may be thinking that the last place you would be going for a sunbathing holiday is the South Pole, so perhaps you need not worry? Unfortunately ozone depletion is not confined to the Antarctic region. See Figure 6.5 for figures for the northern hemisphere. Every year 12,000 people in the USA, and over 1,000 in the UK, die from the most lethal form of skin cancer, malignant melanoma. Many more suffer from non-malignant forms which, nevertheless, require surgical treatment. Australia, with about one-third of the population of the UK, has even more deaths from skin cancer. There is no doubt that skin cancer is the result of exposure to UV radiation and that this effect is more damaging to fair-skinned people than to those with darker skins, so, clearly, anything which increases the UV radiation reaching the Earth's surface is a danger. So what causes a reduction in the ozone of the stratosphere?

The first cause is the UV radiation itself. The reason that ozone blocks the path of UV radiation is that the ozone molecules absorb this radiation. This happens because, when UV radiation strikes a molecule of ozone, the energy absorbed causes the molecule to split up into one molecule of normal oxygen and one single oxygen atom.

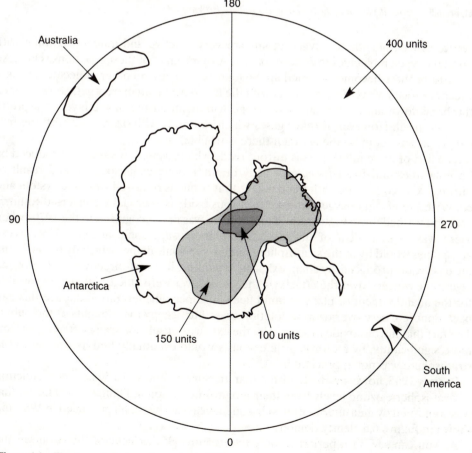

Figure 6.4 *The ozone hole over Antarctica in 1989*

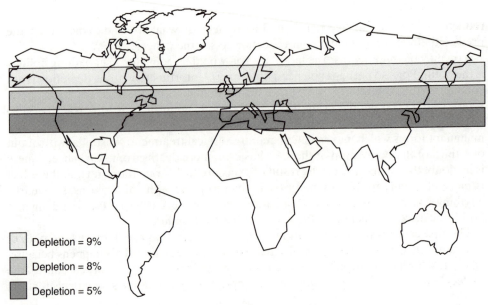

Depletion = 9%

Depletion = 8%

Depletion = 5%

Figure 6.5   *Ozone depletion in the northern hemisphere 1978 to 1990*

As we saw earlier, these oxygen atoms are very reactive and quickly combine with normal oxygen molecules to re-form ozone. A by-product of these reactions is heat, so the stratosphere becomes warmed up. So long as there are no other molecules around, except nitrogen which does not react with the free oxygen but merely gets warmer, then the breakdown and re-formation of ozone will maintain the ozone layer at a pretty constant level. However, if other gases which *can* react with ozone and with the free oxygen atoms get in on the act then there is trouble!

The first of these interlopers is nitrous oxide which, as we have seen, is produced by burning trees and fossil fuels, especially in automobile exhausts. The end result of nitrous oxide combining with the ozone is that ozone is removed from the system and converted to normal oxygen whilst the nitrous oxide is eventually converted to nitric acid and washed down in the rain. This problem was first recognized in the 1970s when there was a great deal of interest in developing supersonic airlines. Since these aeroplanes would fly in the stratosphere, unlike sub-sonic planes which fly below it, the nitrous oxide produced by their exhausts would be injected directly into the ozone layer. The concern over the effects on the ozone layer were at least in part responsible for the abandonment of plans to build fleets of supersonic aircraft and, once this had been done, concern over ozone depletion ceased to occupy the thoughts of the public. The fact that nitrous oxide produced by the exhausts of sub-sonic aircraft and, perhaps more significantly, by motor vehicle exhausts would eventually find its way up to the stratosphere was not appreciated.

In early 1985, however, the British Antarctic Survey reported a 50 per cent reduction in stratospheric ozone levels from their monitoring station at Halley Bay. This finding was confirmed by measurements in subsequent years as the graph produced in 1987 and shown in Figure 6.6 clearly demonstrates.

As you can see, in a period of only two months, 95 per cent of the ozone in the stratosphere disappeared.

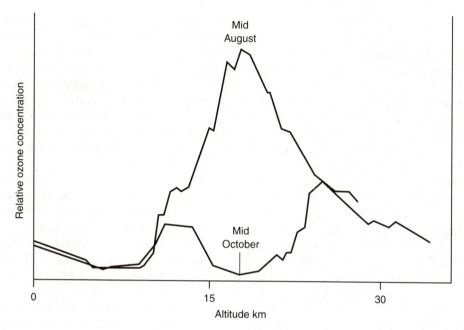

Figure 6.6 *Ozone levels at Halley Bay, Autumn and Spring 1987*

CFCs and the ozone layer

Although prior to this time concern over the ozone layer was limited, in the United States a debate had been raging for some time about the use of CFCs and, as early as 1974, chemists in California had shown that CFCs could destroy stratospheric ozone. As a result of concerns about their long life in the atmosphere and the possible damage they might be causing, their use in aerosols was banned in the USA even before the ozone hole was discovered. This did not, however, apply to their use in the rest of the world.

So why are CFCs so destructive? Although very stable, and insoluble in water, the molecules of CFCs cannot withstand the high energy bombardment by UV radiation they are subjected to once they reach the stratosphere. Here they are broken down and chlorine atoms are released. Now chlorine is a very reactive element and reacts rapidly with ozone to produce a chemical called chlorine monoxide. This, in turn, reacts with some of the free oxygen atoms around to produce normal oxygen and re-release the chlorine. This chlorine can then, of course, start the whole process again, and so ozone breakdown carries on at a very rapid rate. It has been calculated that each atom of chlorine, released from one of the CFCs, can break down 100,000 molecules of ozone!

This was the theory, but it was not until samples taken by NASA's high altitude research aircraft demonstrated a perfect match between the concentration of chlorine monoxide and the reduction in ozone concentration that the link between the ozone hole and CFCs was finally confirmed. So, just as we saw in relation to the greenhouse effect, CFCs turn out to be the major villains at breaking down ozone.

There is no doubt that the discovery of the sudden appearance of the ozone hole caused far more alarm bells to ring than did the slowly accumulating evidence of global warming. This time world governments were stung into action and, in 1987, 20 countries signed the Montreal Protocol under which they pledged a reduction of 50 per cent in CFC emissions by the year 2000. Before governments could sit back and congratulate themselves, however, further research data showed that the problem was far from being solved. Even with a 100 per cent reduction the presence of so many long-lived CFC molecules in the atmosphere would continue to pose a threat to the ozone layer. for at least another 100 years! 50 per cent was just not good enough and the reduction in ozone levels was now detectable in the northern hemisphere.

The results of a further study by NASA released in April 1991 doubled previous estimates of the annual loss of ozone over the northern United States from three per cent per annum to six per cent and showed that the lowest levels persisted until late spring when many people go outdoors more and when growing crops and young animals are most vulnerable to damage from UV radiation. It has been shown that soya bean suffers a 25 per cent decrease in yield if subjected to a 25 per cent increase in UVB radiation and there is evidence of cattle suffering from 'pink eye' where UV radiation has increased. A massive international research programme is now under way into ozone depletion and controls on CFCs are being slowly tightened. But will this bring about improvements before we all have to wear protective clothing before going outdoors and our crops have to be grown under UV absorbing covers?

ACID RAIN

Of course, it might be that we will not have to worry about the effects of UV radiation on our crops because they will have been destroyed earlier by acid rain!

To many people this is seen as a more tangible threat than global warming or the ozone hole. After all, the sight of badly eroded ancient buildings and statues, or vast areas of dead trees in the Black Forest of Germany, or lakes and rivers in Scandinavia in which all the fish have died seems to indicate a much more obvious threat than a hole in an invisible gas over the South Pole!

So what is acid rain? We measure the acidity of something using the pH scale, and a pH of 7.0 is neutral. Anything above this is alkaline and anything below is acid. So the lower the pH reading, the more acid something is.

The atmosphere naturally contains some carbon dioxide and when some of this dissolves in falling rain it forms a dilute solution of carbonic acid. This is a weak acid, but it does lower the pH of normal rain to around 5.6. In areas such as the northeastern United States and Scandinavia the rainfall pH is now usually between 3 and 4, and not infrequently falls below pH 3.0. This may not be strong enough to burn our skin, but it is strong enough to dissolve some of the calcium in the shells of aquatic animals such as crayfish, so weakening them and making them prone to disease. It is strong enough to dissolve nutrients out of the soil, so causing plants to suffer mineral salt deficiencies and to damage the leaves of some plants directly.

Let's see where this acid comes from. You will remember that the end result of nitrous oxide interacting with ozone was that nitric acid was formed and washed down in the rain. Well, we probably all remember from school chemistry that nitric acid is not very nice! Unfortunately, it is joined by a lot of other nasties in the rain to produce a pretty unpleasant cocktail in some places.

Firstly, some of the chlorine released from CFCs is eventually washed back down to the surface, by which time it has combined with water to form hydrochloric acid – remember how nasty that is? But – there is more! The burning of fossil fuels, especially coal, produces oxides of sulphur, such as sulphur dioxide. When this is dissolved in water and washed back to Earth it returns to us as sulphuric acid and its relative, sulphurous acid. So now we have a nice cocktail of all the most corrosive acids from the chemistry lab – nitric, hydrochloric, and sulphuric acids!

During the infamous 'smogs' of London, in the 1950s, rain acidities of 1.6 were recorded, at which levels getting rain in the eyes was certainly quite painful.

The serious health hazard created by this situation was recognized and the burning of coal was severely restricted, so doing much to improve the situation. Controls on industrial emissions causing acid rain are in place in many countries and are improving the situation, especially with regard to the sulphur compounds.

The key cause of acid rain is the input of pollutants from motor vehicles and this has yet to be tackled effectively.

Chapter 7

Motormania Rules, OK?

Figure 7.1 *Cityscape of the 90s?*

Car purchase, car use, lifestyles, and economic activity are intimately linked. Two features that weld them all together are perhaps advertising and our vulnerability as frail, impressionable, and complex social animals.

Take a look at a number of advertisements for cars, especially those on TV, and see what they have in common. Here are a few terms that might help you. How about freedom ... individuality ... seduction ... style ... exuberance for starters? All these ideas are gift-wrapped and targeted at a range of individuals to present them perhaps with images of how they should be living their lives. There are some interesting undercurrents at play here, and these bite deep into human emotions about how we feel about ourselves. Moreover, the images often present a subtle view about how we would like other people to see us. The message is a deceptively simple one. Buy the car – buy the lifestyle.

'Yes, you too can be part of the adventurous off-road set in this fabulous go-anywhere four wheel drive vehicle. Get the go-anywhere spirit and pound your way along green lanes, over muddy fields, and across the most precipitous terrain ... ' The image is attractive but rather absurd. How many people actually need to pound their way along green lanes or over muddy fields? The odd farmer in a hurry perhaps, but the rest of us?

'Yes, you too can turn heads at the local shopping centre when you turn up in your chic little in-town run-around that will park anywhere' – and of course there will inevitably be a suggestion that bigger cars are beaten into submission when the little car just squeezes into the only available parking space. Another attractive image which is confounded by reality. You eventually get into town hot and bothered through a horrendous traffic jam and cannot find anywhere to park. You wind up parking three blocks away and walk through the traffic fumes to arrive at the shops looking a total mess ....

Selling cars is vital to our economy. It is the basis of employment not just for hundreds of thousands of people directly in the vehicle industry itself, but also for the suppliers of garage services, secondhand replacement parts, and accessories, and for the road building and repair business. A cynical view of all of this would include the police, insurance, and legal systems which all rely on road vehicle activity for their 'business'.

Broader aspects of car culture can be a significant factor in the gaining of employ-ment. The 'best' jobs come with a car. Even better it may be a 'status' car and so the manifestations of a superior lifestyle can be portrayed at little, if any, extra personal cost. More to the point, those that have company cars will use them at every opportu-nity for any trivial journey and long ones too – after all they will not pick up the tab for depreciation or maintenance and maybe even fuel as well. Around half of the new car sales in the UK are for company use. A lot of people gain a great deal of low-cost transportation at the expense of everybody else.

To most of us in the developed world, the freedom and complexity of lifestyle we have developed as a result of car use is similar to drug abuse. We enjoy the 'highs' of a liberated go-anywhere do-anything lifestyle. But the price of this addiction is a cryptic 'downer' in which we all share some of the disadvantages of ever-extending car use from noise, pollution, and loss of land space to concrete.

There is also a strange paradox to all of this. The empowerment of us all in extending our own self-will in travelling as we may please, when we please, has happened on a massive scale. As a consequence, with increasing use there has to be increased regulation about where we can park and for how long and how fast we travel and so on. In the end, the paradox leads us to the unfortunate conclusion that as we are able to gain access to more of our environment, that very principle of increased access brings with it environmental destruction, and that includes us.

Personal mobility is not so much an issue as the way in which it is undertaken. The use of language in political circles colours our perception of what is desirable. Large information boards next to new road schemes may proclaim that the Highways Agency on our behalf is 'Investing in Roads'. Talk of public transport, on the other hand, is flavoured with the word 'subsidy'!

Let us look at a few facts.

- It is now generally appreciated that transport is by far the largest drain on global oil reserves.
- At the present rate of extraction, worldwide oil reserves are expected to run out within about 40 years.
- A wide range of chemicals, drugs, plastics, etc. are derived from oil.
- Car fuel economy could be extended to beyond 65 mpg – if the investment was made by the car companies.
- By the year 2000 there are expected to be at least 33 million vehicles on the roads in the UK.
- Between 1988 and 1993 the funding for roads in the UK doubled but in 1991 the UK Minister of Transport announced a new British transport policy emphasizing moving freight transport from road to rail.
- 75 per cent of the Ministry of Transport report on the UK government's spending plans for 1994 referred to roads and only ten per cent to rail.
- In cities, trams are economical, fast, energy-efficient and less environmentally damaging than any other form of powered transport – we deliberately excluded the bike!
- In 1990, road deaths in the UK were estimated to cost the country £6.5 billion per year!

We could go on, but surely the picture is clear by now!

Of course motor vehicles are useful and in some places they are essential, but in many instances there are environmentally better alternatives which will not burn up our rapidly diminishing oil supplies and cause all that pollution. The ways are there, but do we have the will?

Let us take a look at the science behind some of these facts.

As we have seen, road transport is a major user of fossil fuel resources and makes a correspondingly significant contribution to air pollution. As implements of **energy transfer** road vehicles serve to alert us to the wider issues of so-called energy use and ideas on sustainable energy resources. It is worth stepping back at this point and considering the term **energy** itself. In our everyday existence, *everything* that happens is due to energy transfers.

Think back to the start of this book when we considered the energy input into an ecosystem. The Sun shines. The energy transferred from the sunlight is transferred via photosynthesis to new plant tissues. Some of the sunlight is stored as sugars and we would describe this as chemical potential energy. It is energy that could make things 'go' if it had the chance.

Energy transferred to the plant enables chemical reactions to occur. These involve movements of various molecules as new compounds are created and destroyed. So growth, the adding of new tissue to the plant structure, also involves motion. We refer to this motion as kinetic energy – and it can occur on a microscopic or macroscopic scale. So organisms grow then eventually die, decay, and become buried. The decayed remains are later extracted as oil deposits and are seen as a source of potential energy.

These are the fossil fuels and represent a store of the sunlight that beamed down upon the Earth millions of years ago.

The largest store of such fossil fuels on the Earth is in the form of coal, but the most versatile, and valuable, are those deposits which have become stored in a liquefied form. Liquid fossil stores of energy, such as oil, are the mainstay of our transport industry. Refined oil products such as aviation fuels, diesel, and petrol are immensely concentrated stores of potential energy. Let us take the story a little bit further.

Fuels such as petrol are combined with oxygen in car engines. They produce heat and a mass of very hot gases which can be used to apply a force to moving parts such as the pistons in order to make the car move. In energy conversion terms, the potential energy in the fuel is converted to rapidly moving molecules of a range of gases. Yes, back to motion energy again. The moving particles apply a force to the pistons. Here we see an energy transfer in operation – from the microscopic to the macroscopic. The piston is attached via a connecting rod to a bent shaft, called the crankshaft, and from here the motion energy is transferred to the wheels and so propels the vehicle. Again it is the interplay of energy transfers and forces acting which enable this to happen.

OK, so your car is using up petrol, but is it 'using up' energy as is so often said? It is worth reflecting on the use of language and our teaching at this point. In everyday speech we often talk about 'using energy'. From the example with the car engine, it seems reasonable that the energy store – in this case the fossil fuel – is being used up. You put in petrol at the filling station, drive the car, use up the fuel, and then need some more to replace that which has been burnt up. But have you used up the energy? The energy is certainly no longer stored up in the petrol, but has it been 'used up'?

There are two important concepts to bear in mind here. The first concerns the conservation of matter.

It looks as if we have started with something – a few litres of liquid – and ended up with less. After driving all we have got is an empty fuel tank, a bit of soot on the exhaust pipe and some gases puffing out the back. For our purposes, the amount of matter before and after driving is exactly the same. It has merely changed its form from mainly a dense liquid to a spaced out cocktail of gases.

This notion of the conservation of matter we recognize as having a parallel with experiences at a classroom level when we consider activities such as the conservation of volume. Think about the plasticine which is rolled into a ball. Now squash it out thin and flat. Is there more or less than before? But what about energy? Surely there is less energy after the car has been driven?

Not so!

This principle is the conservation of energy and it states that *energy can be neither created nor destroyed*. It also means that for any given situation the total amount of energy before an event is the same as after it.

After the car has been driven where has the energy gone? Or to put it in more accurate terms, to where has the energy been transferred? Most of the energy was never converted into useful movement energy. It was transferred directly into heat that has then been dissipated via the radiator. Petrol engines are notoriously inefficient in this way. Much of the rest has been transferred into heat energy through the rubbing of various moving parts. This includes moving parts in the engine, in the transmission, by the tyres pressing against the road, and by the car body pushing air out of the way so it can move along. We call this rubbing friction and it is simply a term we use to describe forces which oppose motion. So with all this friction where does all the energy go? Rub your hands together and you will quickly discover the answer – it goes to heat. Again, then, the end result is that the energy has been transferred to heat. If you are not convinced, just feel your tyres after a journey, even on a cold day!

Yet more of the energy has been transferred to noise as sound waves move out from the engine and transfer motion to our eardrums! Notice how we are still talking about the interplay of motion and force with which we describe energy transfers. Even the sound waves will end up interacting with particles and causing friction.

And what is heat? Well, a simple description is that it involves particles in motion. This is another expression of kinetic energy. The more the particles move then the higher the temperature. The difference between the kinetic energy of the movement of the car and the kinetic energy of the movement of the molecules involved with heat is that the molecular motion is disordered and random whereas the car's motion is ordered. Heat, as we know, flows from hotter bodies to cooler ones. So the car warms up the air as heat is transferred via the moving parts. The air at ground level warms up the cooler air above. Heat is eventually radiated out into space. No energy has been created in any of this process and none has been lost. The only real change is that from a higher grade fuel with a great deal of potential to make a miniature fiery furnace in the cylinder head, to a low grade heat spread over an incredibly wide area.

We do not use up energy, but we do use up its usefulness.

This idea of the conservation of energy is different from energy conservation. Energy conservation is really about making the most of energy supplies at each stage in their transfer.

In the case of a car for example, it means getting the same litre of fuel to enable the car to go a greater distance than it did previously. Are you surprised to hear that a car could be made to do at least 65 mpg? In the 1940s/1950s you could get around 25 mpg from an average sized family car. If you drove a modern car of the same power at the same speeds – i.e. quite a lot slower – you would expect to get around 40 mpg. This has been achieved partly by more efficient engines, which transfer a higher proportion of the potential energy in the fuel to movement, and partly by reducing the losses due to rubbing friction. More efficient oils, better tyres and, most of all, more aerodynamic shapes, have all contributed to this improvement.

Primary school children can't do much experimenting on energy efficient engines, but they can do a lot of useful investigations into the air and water resistance of different shapes. If they store the same amount of energy in a buggy by twisting an elastic band the same number of times, then see how far this energy store can move the buggy with shapes of different wind resistance, they can make some interesting comparisons with pictures of old and modern cars.

Further improvements in engine design, in particular, could improve the efficiency of energy transfer much more but, if the forecast of 33 million vehicles on UK roads alone comes about, this investment will be running to stand still! Oil reserves will still run out in about 40 years time if we keep burning it up. If we don't drastically reduce oil consumption by motor vehicles we will not only run out of the fuel to drive them but, even more importantly, we will lose the raw materials for all those useful drugs and plastics. This could herald an even greater change in lifestyle than doing without cars!

Of course, not all the oil is used up by running cars. A great deal is used in industry. Perhaps the most telling example is that it takes hundreds of gallons of oil to make one car!

So what are the alternatives?

Well, we could switch to running our cars on gas – LPG (liquid petroleum gas) is quite plentiful, but it is still a fossil fuel and so there are limited reserves. Methane is a better bet as it is produced naturally by waste tips, farm animals, and even termites! But how can it be harnessed for use? Solve that one and you are rich! Alcohol (in the tank not in the driver!) is one of the best options at the present time, and is used extensively in South America already. Cheap alcohol can be produced from many types of organic waste such as wood chippings, sugar cane, and even waste oranges. It requires little modification to the engine, is far less polluting than petroleum products, but is more expensive. Again it is a question of priorities!

Probably most development work has gone into trying to produce a practical electrically driven vehicle. In California, where the zero emission law is looming up, manufacturers have had to take this option seriously and have made significant progress. The major stumbling block is still the development of a lightweight but sufficiently powerful battery. Remember, however, we still have to generate electrical energy and most of this is currently done using fossil fuels – coal, oil, and gas. How much extra electricity generation would be required if we all drove electric cars, and how much extra pollution would that cause? In the USA there have been some studies into this question, and it has been found that the electricity generating companies cause far more pollution from CO_2 than any other branch of industry! See Figure 7.2.

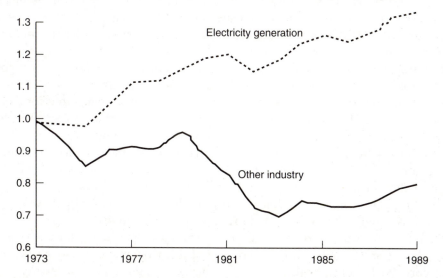

Figure 7.2 *CO_2 pollution by electricity generation and other industries in USA*

There are, however, many cases where road transport is simply not necessary. It could even be said that *most* road transport is simply not necessary.

A train is six times more fuel efficient than a heavy lorry. Trams, as we have seen, are particularly fuel efficient and non-polluting in cities and boats are 100 times more fuel efficient than lorries! In continental Europe canals are still an important mode of transport yet, in the UK, we have allowed our canals to deteriorate so that those that remain are mainly only suitable for, and used by, recreational traffic.

Finally, what about all those accidents? Car manufacturers have spent vast sums of money on crumple zones, tyres with better grip, seat belts, ABS (automatic braking systems), airbags, and so on, all to make cars safer. All this development has paid off, it has worked – cars *are* much safer than they used to be, but the accident rate is still far higher than for any other means of transport, except motorbikes. Riding a pedal cycle and walking are also quite dangerous – but only because you get hit by cars and lorries!

Forget the suffering – count the cost! We could probably wipe out two or three major diseases with the money saved from not having to treat all those road casualties, from lost work hours, re-training costs, and so on.

A SCHOOL'S PERSPECTIVE

What does all of this mean in our teaching? Well, for a start we have to go no further than to look at how children arrive at school, and teachers for that matter. Gone it seems are the years when most children walked to school.

Let's explore a few questions you could ask yourself and your class. How many children in your class travel to school by car? How far do they travel? Is there an alternative, more environmentally friendly mode of transport available? If there is, why don't they use it? How many cars does each family own? How much does it cost to own/ run/maintain these cars?

Car dropping-off points are the norm and congestion around school gates at going-home time is frequently a problem. In discussion with parents it often emerges that children are dropped off at school because it is considered too dangerous for them to walk with all those busy roads to cross, not to mention the odd child molester who lurks in that piece of wasteland by the recreation ground. You will note of course that some of the morning frenzy on the roads is due to parents taking their children to school! If you doubt this try driving along your normal route to work at your normal time of day during half term and you will soon notice the difference that makes!

What happens from here is really up to you. Clearly one mechanism to change the situation is to reduce the amount and speed of the traffic and to encourage children to walk. If the streets are more 'peopled' then there is less opportunity for furtive action by molesters and suchlike. This is again one of the paradoxes of personalized motor transport. Walkers are more at risk of muggings or other personal attacks simply because most of the world passes by on the other side of the kerbstone, in their cars, and ignores what is going on on the pavement.

So what are you going to do?

The children in your class will be growing up in a world where it is not OK for motormania to continue to rule. By the time they are learning to drive that 40-year deadline for oil supplies will be getting closer so they need to start learning about the implications of this now! But you can also take some action yourself. Gaining the support of the headteacher, parents and governors and explaining your needs to the local council is a good starting point. How about some traffic calming measures and sets of pedestrian crossings that actually give priority to those on foot? It may be seen as a political act, but that is up to your conscience ...

Chapter 8

No More Room at the Inn?

POPULATION

Living organisms rarely, if ever, live alone. As we saw earlier, there is normally a range of living things, both plants and animals, living in a particular set of conditions, which we called their habitat. All the various organisms living in one place and carving the habitat up between them are described as a **community**. Within any community, however, you would normally expect to find a number of organisms of the same species, all living together and interacting with each other. Such a single-species group is then called a **population** and the study of populations is called **demography**. There are four major aspects of demography: distribution, growth, movement, and structure. Since this book is mainly concerned with the problems associated with the population of the human species, we will concentrate mainly on the first two of these aspects.

Before we begin, however, let us examine some general ideas about population.

As we saw at the start of this book, all organisms have to find ways of successfully interacting with both their physical and living environments. An important factor in the success of a species will be how well it is able to cope with other components of the environment. In many ways the role of the whole population is of far greater importance than that of its individual members. This is a very important idea for, until relatively recently, biologists tended to think of populations as no more than collections of individuals that happened to be living in the same place. We now appreciate that populations are far more complex than this – knowledge that is just as significant to the study of human populations as to the study of any other species.

Populations take many different forms, and may vary greatly in their size and in their detailed make-up. One of the most significant features of any population, however, is the mechanism which they employ to increase their numbers.

The greatest variation in reproductive methods is to be found in plant species but even animal populations may show some variations from the usual type of sexual reproduction. For example, populations of greenfly (aphids) are able to reproduce very rapidly by using parthenogenesis, the production of offspring without fertilization. This has advantages for greenfly that need to reproduce very rapidly but does not introduce the kind of genetic variation that would, perhaps, enable them to resist an attack by some disease-causing organism. Since all the individuals in such a population are genetically identical, a disease could wipe out the entire population rather as happened with the Irish potato crop, as we saw earlier.

So, in most animal populations sexual reproduction is the norm and this gives rise to a whole range of complex interactions designed to ensure successful fertilization of eggs and the maximum survival rate of the subsequent offspring.

POPULATION DISTRIBUTION

Let us start then with a consideration of population distribution.

If you think back to the topic of trees for a moment, you will remember that the distribution of tree populations was largely determined by climate. The distribution of animal populations typically follows on from the distribution of plants, which form the basis of the food webs in which that animal species feeds. This combination of plant food species at the base of food chains coupled with environmental conditions provides a set of circumstances to which any animal species will be best adapted. Move a species from the conditions to which it is well adapted and it may well soon die out. There are certainly wide variations in the adaptability of different species of both plants and animals but without a doubt the most adaptable species on the Earth is the human species. So let's examine how this species has succeeded in colonizing the available habitats of the Earth.

The surface of the Earth is about 71 per cent water and only 29 per cent land, so less than one third of the Earth's surface has traditionally been available for direct use by humans although there have often been attempts at land reclamation. In more recent years there has been some further exploitation of the areas covered by seas, notably for the extraction of oil, but these uses represent such a small proportion that they are of no significance in terms of population distribution.

People live where they can make a living by farming, mining, industry, etc. and avoid areas where making a living is difficult. Thus we find the world's population is most sparse in areas of desert, and in mountainous and polar regions. About one fifth of the land is desert, another fifth is mountainous and another fifth is too cool. The remaining two-fifths could be farmed or otherwise inhabited, but only a third of this is actually developed. This means, then, that most of the world's population lives on only about 4 per cent of the Earth's surface!

Of course humans have succeeded in colonizing some of the most inhospitable environments on Earth, e.g. the Arctic, Tierra Del Fuego, many deserts, and high mountainous regions. Most, however, have chosen to go where the living is easier! So the largest populations live in four areas, with 34 per cent of the total in the Far East (Japan, China, etc.), 22 per cent in South Asia (India, Pakistan, Bangladesh, etc.), 16 per cent in Europe, the Russian Republics and her neighbours, and 6 per cent in the North East of the USA. There are also several smaller concentrations of population in places such as Indonesia and the Nile delta. The simplified population map below in Figure 8.1 illustrates this pattern.

You have only to think what the climate is like in the various regions of the world to see one reason why people live where they do. The human species may be able to

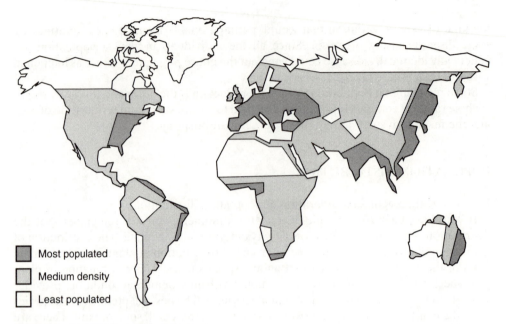

Figure 8.1   *Simplified population distribution map*

colonize the inhospitable parts of the globe but, like all other species, the favoured distribution corresponds to the most favourable climatic conditions.

Such generalized maps of population distribution do not, however, display the total picture. A closer examination of population distribution within the various major zones would show, for example, that in 1950 slightly more than one quarter of the world's population lived in towns of one sort or another; that is, these people were 'urbanized'. According to recent United Nations' estimates, however, this figure will have risen to almost half the world population by the year 2000. Thus the number of people urbanized may have risen to as many as 2.8 billion! Again, this distribution is far from evenly spread, as the following table, taken from UNCED's *Our Common Future*, The Brundtland Report (OUP, 1987) shows.

Table 8.1   *Population distribution in developed and developing world regions*

Year	1950	1985	2000
World Total	29.2%	41.0%	46.6%
Developed regions	53.8%	71.5%	74.4%
Developing regions	17.0%	31.2%	39.3%

Reproduced by permission of Oxford University Press

It is important to remember this distribution in order to understand many of the problems created by urbanization. Let us at this point take just a few examples of the uneven nature of population distribution.

In 1991 Mexico City had a population of over 19 million whilst in 1990 Bangkok had a population of over eight million. Many of the inhabitants of both cities suffered deprivation but this was far worse in Mexico City than in relatively affluent Bangkok. At around the same time, Bangladesh had a largely impoverished population of around 120 million yet the population of Holland, with a similar overall population density, were by and large prosperous. No doubt, if the population of Bangladesh was 12 million instead of 120 million, all the inhabitants would be able to live in greater comfort on the higher, fertile ground away from the low-lying flood plains, which have seen such catastrophic and regular flooding.

So why, then, is that other low-lying country, Holland, so much better off? Unlike Bangladesh, Holland is an advanced industrialized nation that depends heavily on resources imported from the rest of the world. It could not survive at its present level of prosperity if it had to rely on its own resources to supply the population and did not have the wealth to maintain expensive flood defences. The fundamental problem is obviously not simply one of numbers, but rather of the relationship between economics and population numbers.

Two factors contribute to changes in population levels: emigration/immigration, and natural increase/decrease.

Population movements

We do not propose to dwell on the results of population movements other than to relate it to population growth.

A common cause of population change in a particular area is that the population has become too large for the available resources. Overcrowding and food shortage result and one way out of the situation is for some of the population to move away in search of more space and moor food. These were probably the reasons why the first human populations spread out and one of these factors, food shortage, was of course the reason why so many Irish emigrated to the United States. In more recent times, large human population movements are more likely to be due to political or cultural factors.

Today, with the free movement of people within the European Union (EU) you might expect the pattern of population growth to change. However, such changes as have taken place are unlikely to be mainly due to population mobility.

So immigration and emigration will affect the population of individual countries as, for example, was mentioned in relation to the Irish potato famine when the USA gained and Ireland lost population during the last century. Immigration and emigration does not, however, change the total world population.

Population growth

The problems of cities such as Mexico City and regions like Bangladesh do not, however, stop at the current population level. Far more serious is the rate of population growth in these areas and this we will turn to next.

All species are capable of reproducing their own kind and this ability is one of the key factors in defining signs of life. It is, of course, also a fact that all living things will eventually die, so the continuance of the species is dependent upon the ability to reproduce. Natural increase results when the birth rate is higher than the death rate, while natural phenomena such as predation, disease, disasters such as earthquakes and even wars – if war can be considered a natural phenomenon – contribute to a natural decrease in populations.

If all the offspring were to survive, then any pair of animals would need only to produce two offspring in their lifetime to ensure survival of the species. In practice, of course, this survival rate is not achieved by any species, even ourselves. So animals have to produce extra offspring to make up for the potential losses. The problem is that the replacement numbers must be produced before the losses are known! The rate of reproduction in any species is dependent upon the lifestyle of that species and this rate has been adjusted over the evolutionary period of the species to compensate for the losses experienced in its past history. Natural selection has weeded out individuals that produced too few or too many offspring. This mechanism of predicting losses is certainly based on far more data than any forecast of the outcome of a national lottery, but it is still only a prediction!

So we find that fish whose eggs and young fry are the favourite food of many other water dwelling animals produce large numbers of eggs. A cod produces around four million eggs at each laying, of which very few will survive. Small rodents such as mice and voles and, of course, rabbits are also near the bottom of the food chain and are preyed upon by stoats, foxes, owls, and many other carnivores. A mouse or a rabbit will typically produce about 30 offspring per year. Even so, this number is small compared to fish because mammals not only protect the eggs and developing embryos inside their bodies before birth, but also protect them in the nest until they are old enough to fend for themselves. By contrast the fox has fewer enemies (very few if you exclude humans), is capable of offering more protection to the young, and produces only around five offspring per year.

In the examples cited so far, any protection of the young has been by the parent or parents of the animals only. In many populations, however, this protection is taken further by being extended to other members. This occurs in populations of antelope, baboons and lions for example.

Where the parent animals, and their offspring, have no significant threat from predators, again apart from humans, which usually means they are very large, then the number of offspring can be reduced even further. Thus the largest land animals, elephants, and largest aquatic animals, whales, only produce one animal at a time and may not breed every year. In both these cases the population takes a role in protecting the young, so whilst a hyena will occasionally manage to take a baby rhino, young elephants will be protected by the whole herd, which will gang up to see off any marauding hyena.

Where the young have such a good chance of survival the adults do not need to start to breed until they are quite old, so elephants do not reach sexual maturity until they are 20 years of age. However, elephants live for around 60 years so they still have the potential to produce far more offspring than are needed to ensure the survival of the species.

From what we have said above you may have recognized two basic strategies for survival:

- Produce large numbers of offspring, let them take their chances and a few will survive to maintain the population level.
- Produce few offspring that will be well protected to ensure that sufficient survive to maintain the population level.

Superimposed upon these two basic strategies, however, we see another effect operating. We are sure that you are familiar with the stories about the population of lemmings growing too large and then large numbers committing suicide by leaping off cliffs. Not quite true, but it is certainly the case that small rodents such as lemmings do over-produce in good times, leading to a population boom. This population boom thus produces a glut of available food for carnivores from owls to stoats to domestic cats. This in turn means that more of these predators' young will survive, indeed usually that more will be born. Not only does this result in additional predation of the original 'boom' species, but these plant eaters will soon exhaust their food supply. With the onset of less favourable conditions, perhaps the winter, or a period of drought, the population numbers collapse, often much faster than they rose in the first place. This boom and bust strategy is typical of animals that produce a great many offspring in a short time.

It might seem that animals which produce few offspring, each with a high chance of survival, would not be subject to this 'boom and bust' principle. However, if we look at the African Elephant as a prime example of the 'few and protected' strategy, we can see that the problem of population is not as clear cut as it might at first seem.

Elephants are highly destructive of their environment for they are selective feeders and will break down whole trees to reach the leaves they want to eat. They also dig for water and do even more damage. So long as the elephant population remains stable, and they are able to roam and feed over a large area, this lifestyle is sustainable. The opening up of the environment will allow new plants access to light and, once the elephants have moved on, the damage will be quickly repaired.

These days elephants no longer have the whole African continent to roam over; they are confined to national parks. This would pose no threat to the environment so long as the elephant population remained small enough to be maintained within the land area available. However, we now realize that elephant populations are not stable. Because of their highly protective breeding strategy and their longevity the population inexorably rises. In the past, what probably happened was that the rising population did destroy their food supply and so elephant numbers suffered a disastrous collapse through starvation.

In fact, then, elephant populations may operate on the same 'boom and bust' strategy as small rodents or even greenfly! Even if there was not this rise in the population large herds could only survive when they were able to move away from the areas they had decimated and not return for many years, after the habitat had recovered.

If we now look at these mechanisms of population control in relation to the behaviour of our own species we will soon recognize some similarities.

Our species consists of relatively large, powerful animals that reach sexual maturity quite late, live a long time, produce few, heavily protected offspring, and use a population-based defence strategy.

The 'slash and burn' process adopted by some farmers is very like the moving-on strategy of elephants. Just as with the elephants, this will only work if there is a vast area in which to move around so that the land can recover before the farmers return. If farmers are confined to a limited area, just like the elephants in national parks, then the strategy fails.

Because we have developed such an ability to control our environment, we have generally been far less susceptible to the 'boom and bust' effect than other animals. The exceptions are when vast numbers of people have been crowded together in towns, which have then been swept by a disease of epidemic proportions. Epidemics such as the Black Death or bubonic plague in the past, or more recent influenza epidemics, do look suspiciously like boom and bust controls operating. Other examples are natural disasters such as the droughts in Africa. It has even been suggested that major wars have operated in the same way as population controls. However, with our ever-increasing control over disease and the potential of technology for alleviating, if not eliminating, natural disasters such as drought, the boom and bust strategy for population control seems less and less likely to operate for our species. Inexorable population rise does seem to have been a problem of the human species for a long time.

The fundamental problem of natural population increase was identified two centuries ago by the mathematician Thomas Malthus, who predicted the fall of the human race because he could not see how food production could keep pace with the rate of population growth. Malthus pointed out that populations have the potential to increase by geometric progression. A geometric progression is one in which the numbers keep doubling like this: 1 – 2 – 4 – 8 – 16 – 32. This is the sort of formula which banks and building societies use to calculate compound interest and which results in a rapidly rising rate of interest as time passes. Fine if you are gaining the interest, but not so good when you are paying it!

If you plot a graph of this progression – see Figure 8.2 – you can easily see how the rate of increase soon reaches an almost vertical rise.

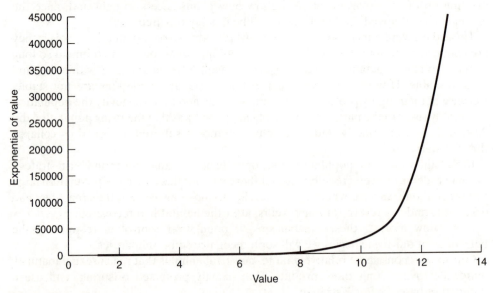

Figure 8.2   *An exponential growth graph*

Thus, in the process of **exponential** growth, the population will double over a given time period, regardless of the starting point.

At present the world population is increasing steadily at about two per cent per annum. Within individual countries, however, there are wide variations from this norm. Very high rates are found in developing countries such as Nigeria with 3.3 per cent per annum and Mexico with 2.6 per cent per annum, whereas developed countries such as the USA with 0.7 per cent per annum and the UK with 0.1 per cent per annum show much lower than average rates. In Germany where people have chosen to have smaller families the population is actually falling, thus giving a negative population growth rate of –0.2 per cent per annum.

The average population growth rates throughout the world during the 1980s are summarized in the diagram in Figure 8.3.

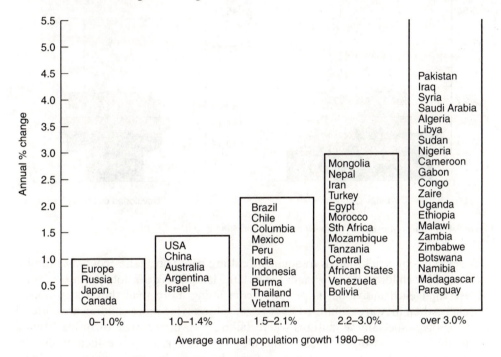

Figure 8.3 *Average annual population growth, 1980–1989*

Where do these differences come from? Well it seems obvious that the birth rate is higher in the areas where people are poorer. Biologically one would expect from the evidence of other animal populations that poorer and thus less well-fed populations would be less fertile and thus have less offspring. This, of course, is where human populations change the rules!

The factors that determine the birth rates in human populations are far more likely to be social than biological ones. Certainly, when economic conditions in a country worsen, there is usually a fall in the birth rate, as happened in the USA during the years of the great depression of the 1930s. This was, however, probably more associated with the economic problems of bringing up a family than with any fall in biological fertility.

One biological factor that certainly does have an effect on birth rate is the age structure of the population. In prosperous, Western countries the age structure shows a much higher proportion of older people than in poorer, developing countries. This is clearly shown in the illustration in Figure 8.4 below.

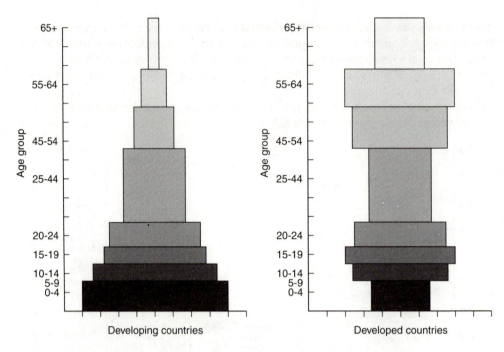

Figure 8.4   *Population pyramids of developed and developing countries*

In developing countries there is frequently a culture based on a false economic premise that sees more children as more hands to work the land. This does not take into account the fact that each individual is probably consuming more than they can produce, especially when they are children. Other reasons for having more children are cultural and religious, especially in cultures where failure to produce male offspring bears a social stigma. This is often allied to the idea that men must prove their virility by producing more children. In countries where the emancipation of women has proceeded further there is normally a marked fall in the birth rate due to these cultural effects. Raised birth rates in developing countries can also be exacerbated by the earlier age at which girls first become pregnant. This is compounded by a tendency to have even more children to overcompensate for the high infant mortality rate. Last, but not least, access to effective contraceptive methods are not so readily available, so women will commonly give birth every year of their sexually active life. Generally, it is the more prosperous and better fed populations that have the lowest birth rates so this is clearly the result of social controls rather than biological ones.

Perhaps the most telling way to illustrate the rate of human population growth would be to plot the changes that have taken place during our history. Unfortunately this is far from easy! The earliest accurate population census was that taken in the USA in 1790. In the UK the first reliable census was not taken until 1841. Certainly the Domesday Book, completed in England in 1086, did attempt a complete census, but this was done in order to assess taxes. Not surprisingly, then, many people avoided being recorded in the Domesday Book! So even that census is not very accurate. Earlier records are very scattered and often based on unreliable sources, so much of the estimates of early population sizes are very speculative.

In his book *Population, Resources, Environment* (Freeman & Co., San Francisco, 1970), Paul Ehrlich, an ecologist at Stanford University, explains how he came to estimate some early population sizes:

> We believe that agriculture was unknown before about 8000 BC. Prior to that date all human groups made their living by hunting and gathering. No more than 20 million square miles of the Earth's total land area of 58 million square miles could have been successfully utilized in this way by our early ancestors. From the population densities of the hunting and gathering tribes of today, we can estimate that the total human population of 8000 BC was about five million people.

Looking at the best estimates various authorities such as Ehrlich have made of past population levels reveals the pattern shown in Figure 8.5.

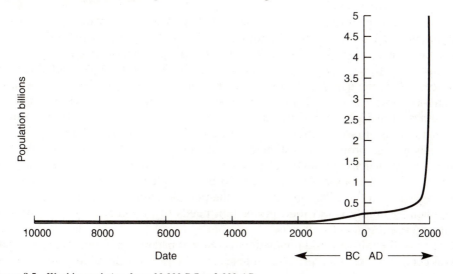

Figure 8.5 *World population from 10,000 BC to 2,000 AD*

A quick look at this graph reveals how close it is to the shape of the exponential graph. Malthus's predictions about the fall of the human race might be proved right in the longer term if this rate of population growth is not controlled. Figures for world population increases show, however, that the population is actually increasing more rapidly than Malthus predicted. The curve is actually 'super exponential'. So the problem is, in reality, even worse than we first thought.

If we know the percentage growth rate of a population, then we can calculate the numbers expected in any given time period. At the present time, as we have seen, there is an annual world increase of 2.0 per cent. This means that the world population will be doubled in the space of only 35 years. With a current world population of five-and-a-half thousand million this means between six and seven thousand million by the end of the century – seven billion people! It does not then take much imagination to see how the figure of forty billion by the end of the twenty-first century, mentioned in the chapter on food, was arrived at.

The world population grew only very slowly until 1750 because natural checks such as disease on epidemic scales, famine and war, coupled with very high infant mortality rates, kept this growth down in spite of high birth rates. Since 1750 the rate of growth has increased considerably. Several factors account for this. In Britain, for example, after 1750 we experienced the Industrial Revolution and populations became attracted away from subsistence agriculture towards the newly developing industrial towns. In time, improved sanitation and medical and social services were made available through innovation and so the infant mortality rate, in particular, fell. The main effect was that the number of children surviving after birth increased beyond the death rate in the population at large. The Industrial Revolution, which had first begun in Britain, spread to Europe and North America which thus saw similar rises in population.

Many other areas of the world have only been introduced to large scale development this century and so these developing countries are experiencing a rapid rise in the rate of population increase. Meanwhile, the developed countries are experiencing a fall in the rate of population growth.

Such an overall population increase is going to have a major effect on practical needs such as food supplies, raw materials, housing, and land. Population growth also affects almost every major social problem: urban overcrowding, rural poverty, unemployment and under-employment, malnutrition, pollution, and the depletion of limited natural resources. While the demands on our global resources made every day by the world's five-and-a-half thousand million consumers are rapidly increasing, it is the rich countries with their increasingly sophisticated lifestyles which consume over 80 per cent of these natural resources, yet they occupy only 20 per cent of inhabited land.

Already a large proportion (estimates vary from 15 to 50 per cent) of the world's population, particularly in the developing countries, is undernourished and many are on the verge of starvation. One only has to be reminded of scenes of starvation in northern Africa in the 1980s and 1990s. If the population is to double in the next 35 years, then obviously world food production needs to be doubled as well, even to maintain present inadequate levels.

Reviewing the rate of world population increase, it becomes apparent that, for areas such as central Africa, food production to sustain the growing population would need to double in around 20 years. No matter what advances may take place in the next 20 years in, say, crop production or irrigation, there is simply no chance that such an enormous rate of increase in food production could take place there.

Clearly, Malthus was right: current, and even future, levels of food production cannot keep pace with present levels of population increase.

It has been suggested that, if agriculture were to operate worldwide at the sort of efficiencies currently operating in the developed countries, then it could support a world population of some 20 billion. In practice, this worldwide efficiency could never be achieved. We have to take into account practical and climatic factors as well as degradation of the environment from pollution, possible losses from rises in sea level, and other effects of the impact of global warming.

Food is not the only problem. As the population rises, so does demand for fuel, metals, land, timber, etc. Many of these resources are finite and non-renewable and are now being used up very rapidly. Increased population also seems to result inevitably in environmental destruction through increased pollution, destruction of wildlife, spread of deserts, destruction of woodlands, and overuse of rural areas for recreation. Problems posed by the pressure of population increase will strain political, social, and economic foundations, particularly between the rich and poor nations of the world. Such pressure leads to increasing risks of war and terrorism and racial tensions.

Taking all these factors into account, experts such as Paul Ehrlich and Michael Soule at the University of Michigan have calculated that the present world population of five-and-a-half billion cannot be sustained indefinitely, let alone the seven billion expected by the end of the century. They suggest that the best we can hope for is a 'holding operation' for the next 500 or so years until our human population reduces sufficiently to take the pressure off our environment.

More than two decades ago, Paul Ehrlich was warning:

> The explosive growth of the human population is the most significant terrestrial event of the past million millennia .... No geological event in a billion years – not the emergence of mighty mountain ranges, nor the subsidence of entire sub-continents, nor the occurrence of periodic glacial ages – has posed a threat to terrestrial life compared to that of human overpopulation. (Paul Ehrlich, *The Population Book* (Ballantine, 1971))

Have we learned nothing since then?

So what solutions are there to all these problems? The only long-term solution must lie in population control, that is slowing down and eventually halting population growth. If the rest of the world was able to follow the example of Germany, which you may remember has experienced a fall in population, then the rise in world population would be halted and should stabilize at around eight billion by 2030 and would probably stay at this level for another 500 years. This would only work, however, if the average birth-rate per female worldwide remained at 2.1 or less.

At various times and in different parts of the world the following methods of reducing population increase have been used or advocated: birth control, sterilization, abortion, infanticide, euthanasia, and government legislation limiting the number of children a couple may have. There are moral, practical, and other objections to each.

The objections to birth control, sterilization, and abortion are often perceived as primarily based on religious and moral grounds. However, all these practices also require money, education and, especially in the latter two methods, medical resources and expertise. Moreover, in those countries where the need is greatest, the lack of a well-developed infrastructure of transport, communication, and social services of all kinds makes the implementation of any of these methods of population limitation difficult.

Traditional tribal groups do seem to have used population control methods usually based on abortion, infanticide, and the prevention of marriage or sexual intercourse.

Abortion raises violent passions in modern societies to the extent that, in America, workers in abortion clinics and hospitals have been attacked and even killed by abortion opponents. However, 99 per cent of tribal societies known to anthropologists practise abortion and this is probably the commonest method of birth control ever used by humans. In pre-Christian Europe abortion was legal and was widely practised by the Greeks and Romans.

Infanticide, the killing of newborn infants, seems to have been widespread throughout the world before the advent of Christianity and remained a common practice in many Australian, American, and African tribes until quite recently. Sometimes more than half of the children born were killed in this way. Thus in the Narrinyeri tribe of Australia every child born before the one preceding it could walk was destroyed.

Euthanasia was also commonly practised in some tribes although the elderly people were less commonly killed, but rather were sent out of the village where they would starve to death. Both these methods are generally considered so morally reprehensible that, as a matter of policy, they cannot be considered as serious options in civilized society.

In most tribes young men are not allowed to marry until they have reached a required level of physical fitness and skill. This ensures that they will be able to support a family to the accepted standard of the tribe. In other societies a similar result is achieved by requiring a large payment to the bride's family thus ensuring that the prospective husband is sufficiently wealthy to support his family. Among the Brahmins of Southern India, only the eldest son and one daughter are allowed to marry thus limiting population increase but also avoiding the dividing up of the landowners' estates. Some African tribes ban intercourse for two years after the birth of a child.

In all these cases the tribal or family control on individuals is powerful enough to ensure that the rules are strictly adhered to.

In modern times population control has been attempted in China via government legislation. Here, benefits are withdrawn if more than one child is born. It remains to be seen if such totalitarian controls are effective. If seems unlikely that the population in a democratic state would vote for such draconian measures.

In the end it would seem that the only hope for the future would be for countries to adopt more environmentally sound economic and social development policies and to encourage smaller families, while at the same time providing access to birth control facilities for those who are prepared to use them. This, as we have seen, is what has happened in Germany, but here we are dealing with a prosperous and well-educated population. The problem is surely that this has only been achieved after the improvements in economic and social conditions, yet in the developing countries the attainment of these conditions will be hindered, if not altogether prevented, unless population growth can be controlled. Undoubtedly this must be the ultimate 'chicken and egg' problem!

Above all, then, there is a need for education about the effects of population growth, for population control, and for improved methods of food production. The problems of food production, conservation, and pollution we have examined are all important in themselves but, without some control on the ever-increasing tide of human population, attempts to tackle these other problems will be doomed to failure.

Chapter 9

Looking to the Future

One of the most influential publications of the environmental movement must have been *The Limits to Growth* (Dennis H. Meadows *et al*, Potomac Associates, 1972). This book set out to examine the possible effects of accelerating industrialization, rapid population growth, malnutrition, depletion of non-renewable resources, and the deterioration of the environment. The concerns raised were supported by the United Nations and the then Secretary-General, the late U Thant, suggested that there were less than ten years in which to forge a global partnership of nations to solve these problems. As we now know, these problems are still far from solved.

However in 1972 there was also held the first international conference on the environment in Stockholm and this, together with the impact of *The Limits to Growth* and various United Nations initiatives has led to many further attempts to develop the global partnership which U Thant envisaged.

Another benchmark in this process was the setting up of the United Nations Commission on Environment and Development (UNCED), which began its deliberations in 1983 and which has spawned several important conferences since. Perhaps the most important of these, certainly in political terms, was the United Nations Conference on Environment and Development held at Rio de Janeiro in June 1992 and commonly known as the 'Earth Summit' conference. At these meetings and conferences the issues raised again and again were exactly the same ones as had been identified two decades earlier in *The Limits to Growth*. At least, at the Rio summit, some agreements were signed that, although not binding, did put governments under some pressure to negotiate for stronger commitments in the future.

Although the youth organizations and the NGOs (non-governmental organizations) associated with the Rio summit were bitterly disappointed at the lack of positive proposals for action, others felt that it may have sown the seeds of a global awareness which could, in turn, lead towards a sustainable future.

In this final chapter we will consider the two alternative scenarios represented by these two views of the Earth summit. Firstly, we will examine some of the predictions which have been made about the future conditions of the global environment if no action is taken on the issues raised at the Rio summit. Secondly, we will consider the more hopeful options for a sustainable future.

THE DOOMSDAY SCENARIO

Views of the future have often proved to be notoriously unreliable so perhaps it is safer to talk about trends rather than absolutes in anything which involves our own actions.

This first scenario we may identify as simply 'carry on as you are'. This sounds fairly reasonable since in our moderately green and pleasant land the air is still breathable and the raised sea levels from threatened global warming are hardly lapping at the doorstep. Within this trend, however, many developing countries are carrying on as they are, and this may mean massive erosion of natural environments and a growth of energy usage from unsustainable sources.

Take India as an example. Here for centuries many people have led low energy lifestyles and used biomass fuels such as cow dung for their everyday needs. But aspirations change. In an ever growing population there is going to be an increasing number of people who wish to gain access to the technological riches of the developed world. A pile of cow dung will hardly help run a computer. India is emerging as one of the leaders in the 'Carbon Club' as some of the greatest stocks of coal are now being conveyed into power station furnaces to feed the growing demand for that versatile power source, electricity. 'Carry on as you are' in India is not a matter of stabilizing anything, it is continuing with an insatiable industrial growth culture. This, of course, is exactly the first problem identified by *The Limits to Growth* two decades ago!

Moreover, many in India would claim that until the developed countries of the world have put their environmental house in order, they should not criticize those in other lands that simply want to catch up with the West. And, of course, they have a very valid point. As Gro Harlem Brundtland, Chair of the UNCED, said: 'It is both futile and an insult to the poor to tell them they must live in poverty to protect the environment' (*Our Common Future*, The Brundtland Report, UNCED, 1987).

We can use the industrial aspirations of India as a starting point for our examination of some 'doomsday' predictions and we will start with the possible results of the burning of all that coal.

As we have seen already, burning fossil fuels is the greatest contributor to the increase of carbon dioxide in the atmosphere. We have also reviewed some of the evidence to show that carbon dioxide, together with other greenhouse gases, such as the CFCs and HCFCs, is causing enhanced global warming and that this warming is causing melting of Antarctic ice.

As we said at the start of this section, in looking to the future there are no certainties and this is why scientists prefer to talk of 'projections' rather than 'predictions'. There are, however, some hard facts to go on. There is no doubt that the greenhouse effect is a fact – without it the surface temperature of the Earth would average minus 19 degrees Celsius instead of the plus 15 Celsius we actually enjoy! So there is a warming of 34 degrees Celsius due to the effect of the 'natural' greenhouse gases: water vapour, carbon dioxide, and methane in particular. What is also certain is that the concentrations of greenhouse gases in the atmosphere have increased significantly since the Industrial Revolution, as the following table shows.

Table 9.1

	Carbon dioxide	Methane	Nitrous oxide	CFCs	HCFCs
Concentrations ppm in 1795	279	790	285	0	0
Concentrations ppm in 1990	354	1,720	310	760	320

ppm = parts per million

There is no agreement amongst the experts as to what the effect of this increase in greenhouse gases will be, although it is now generally accepted that emissions of all greenhouse gases should be initially stabilized at present levels and then progressively reduced.

So what do the pessimists say may happen if this reduction does not take place, and preferably much sooner than present governments envisage?

The usual way to try to assess the effects is to consider what would happen if the concentrations of greenhouse gases doubled, and this is usually worked out for carbon dioxide. Such calculations lead to a projection that a doubling of carbon dioxide levels would cause a temperature rise of between three and six degrees Celsius. It doesn't sound a lot, but it would take global temperatures much higher than they have been for several million years! But how long would it take for carbon dioxide levels to double and so cause this temperature rise?

Again estimates vary widely, with the pessimists estimating a doubling by around 2040 and the optimists suggesting as long as 2100. What does seem certain is that temperatures *will* rise – it is just that we don't know by how much and how fast. OK, so temperatures are going to rise. Warmer summer holidays, faster crop growth, lower heating bills – a Mediterranean climate in Manchester no less! Unfortunately, anything to do with climate is not that simple!

The first point to bear in mind is that higher temperatures mean more evaporation. More evaporation will have two effects. Firstly, some areas of the world will become much drier: soil moisture content will go down and so any increased plant growth due to temperature would be wiped out because the plants would not have sufficient water. This particular effect is most likely to be felt in the northern hemisphere. This is because there is a greater land mass than the southern hemisphere, and land heats up faster than water. In fact, the models suggest that the further north you go, the faster will be the rate of warming. Probably the area to be hit hardest by such a change would be North America and this could have serious implications for world food supplies.

The following map in Figure 9.1 shows predictions made for some areas of the USA.

At present America exports vast amounts of grain but a change to a drier climate could result in the need to import, instead of export, grain. With this scenario in mind, various attempts have been made to project the effects of a drier climate on many sites in the USA. Amongst the results obtained are suggestions that the Great Lakes could

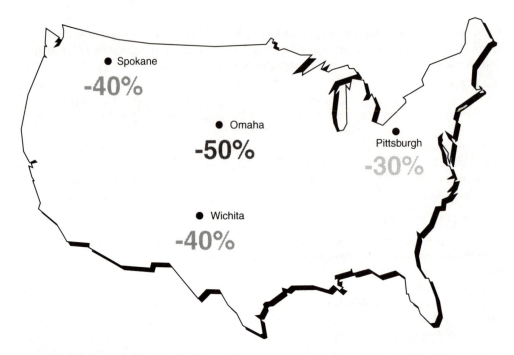

Figure 9.1   *Projected soil moisture decrease from 1986 levels*

fall by anything between 0.6 and 2.4 metres and river flows in the western states could be cut drastically, as shown in the following chart in Figure 9.2.

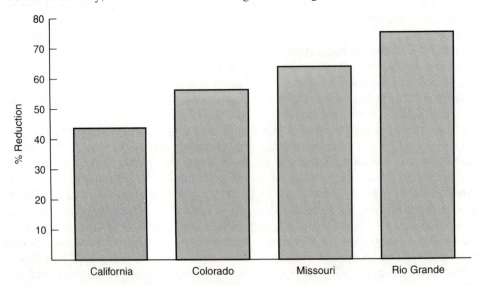

Figure 9.2   *Projected reduction in flow of some US rivers*

Furthermore, grain harvests in the Midwest could fall by 30 per cent and it has even been suggested that the great Midwest grain belt could move up into northern Canada!

Of course, many will say it could never happen, but situations rather like this did occur in 1988 when the USA had the hottest, driest summer in living memory with crop failures, the Mississippi so low that barge traffic was stranded, water rationing in California, and massive forest fires in Yellowstone National Park. At the same time as all this was happening in the northern hemisphere, Bangladesh had the worst floods in memory – just what the climate models predict would happen in the southern hemisphere as the northern hemisphere became drier!

Warmer oceans, however, may have even more serious consequences. In particular, they cause more intense storms. According to the National Hurricane Center in Miami, Florida, 1990 was the most active year on record for hurricanes in both the Atlantic and the Pacific. In 1992 Hurricane Andrew set new records for devastation and the massive damage claims put some insurance companies out of business.

So let's move from the northern to the southern hemisphere and see what global warming might have in store. In 1992 a large-scale UN-backed study in Indonesia, Malaysia and Thailand examined the possible effects of a doubling of carbon dioxide in the atmosphere between 2050 and 2060 – a fairly conservative estimate. The researchers assumed the 'carry on as you are' scenario, in which nothing is done to reduce carbon dioxide levels. On this basis, temperature rises of three degrees Celsius for Indonesia, three to four degrees for Malaysia, and three to six degrees for Thailand were calculated. The results of such rises suggested that some parts of the region could suffer a doubling of rainfall and an increase in the incidence of tropical cyclones. This would only be a continuance of the pattern already observed by the Miami Hurricane Center. Whilst the increased rainfall might appear to offer advantages for agriculture, it seems more likely that this would be more than negated by increased soil erosion – with anything from 14 to 40 per cent of the topsoil being lost – and serious leaching out of soil nutrients. Overall soil fertility could be reduced by between two and eight per cent resulting in huge losses of production of crops such as soya bean. Some crops, such as maize, would be directly harmed by rising temperatures – 'thermal stress' – and, in parts of Indonesia for example, this could cut maize yields by up to 65 per cent.

There has already been a fall in worldwide grain production from a peak in 1980, and projections based on the effects of the expected level of global warming show this downward trend continuing, as the chart in Figure 9.3 indicates.

One of the most damaging effects of global warming, predicted in the South East Asia study, was of widespread flooding. In the southern areas of Java, for instance, rising sea levels could cut rice production by 90 per cent. Not only this, but fishing and shrimp harvesting would be devastated, wiping out the living of as many as 15,000 families in this one area alone. The issue of rising sea levels is potentially one of the most devastating effects of global warming, and this was recognized at the Berlin Climate conference in 1995. Measurements show that, since 1900, sea levels have risen by 100 to 150 millimetres. If the present rate of global warming is not halted then the seas could rise a further 500 millimetres – half a metre – by the year 2100! So concerned are many low-lying countries about this threat that they have formed the Alliance of Small Island States (AOSIS) to press for a 20 per cent reduction in carbon dioxide emissions by 2005. Islands such as the Maldives in the Indian Ocean, the Marshall Islands in the Pacific, Jamaica in the Caribbean, and Cyprus in the Mediterranean could be inundated by rising sea levels and increased tropical storms if the worst case predictions were to come about. Of course, it is not only these small island states that

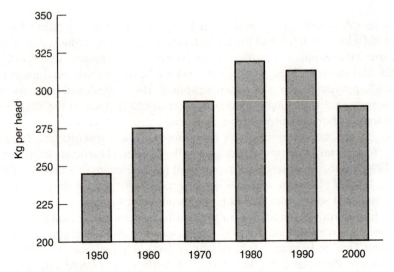

Figure 9.3 *World grain production (kg of grain per head of population)*

would suffer from flooding. Many countries rely heavily on income from tourist resorts based on their coasts, and these would be the first to go.

As the following map, based on the UN IPCC Report, shows in Figure 9.4, even a highly developed country like the Netherlands could be at risk.

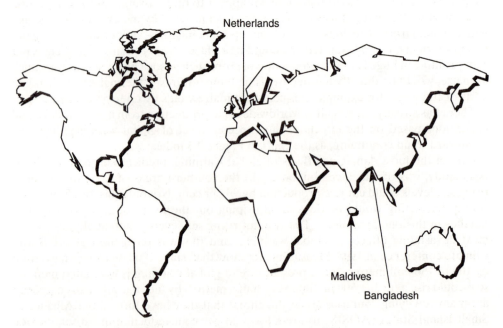

Figure 9.4 *Countries facing flooding from a 60cm rise in sea level*

The AOSIS nations have some support from the countries of the EU, which want to negotiate new targets for carbon dioxide emission, although some of these countries, including the UK, are dragging their feet on this issue. Ranged against those who want controls are the OPEC countries – the oil producers – who are doing everything they can to block any reduction in carbon dioxide emission for purely selfish, financial gain. These OPEC countries are demanding the right to veto any agreement that threatens oil exports and even claiming that global warming is due to sunspots or deforestation rather than carbon dioxide emission. Meanwhile, countries such as China and India go on emitting more and more carbon dioxide into the atmosphere and are doing nothing, saying that global warming is all the fault of the developed Western countries, so they are the ones who have to solve the problem. Is it any wonder that some people are pessimistic about the future!

You may be wondering why rising temperatures with increased evaporation should cause flooding. Well, if you think back to what we said about the melting of the Antarctic ice and the implications of the breaking up of three Antarctic ice shelves in four years, you can see where some of the extra water is coming from. It is the ice shelves which help insulate the Antarctic ice cap from the warmer seas surrounding it. This ice cap, which is 3600 metres thick, contains 70 per cent of the world's fresh water. If this were to melt it would cause the sea to rise by 70 to 180 metres.

Of course, the Antarctic ice shelf is not the only source of rising sea levels. There is a lot of ice in the Arctic, in glaciers, in the permafrost, and on mountains which feed into various rivers. The problem lies not so much in the amount of water being released from any one of these sources, but in what happens when all these smaller amounts are added together.

The amount of the Earth's surface currently covered by ice is really very large, as shown below in Figure 9.5. Try not to worry, but how far do you live above sea level?!

In many ways the greatest danger from global warming lies less in the threats we may be able to predict than in those which may be unexpected. For example, recent studies on the Odden feature off Greenland show that the Gulf Stream may weaken. This would result in Britain and northern Europe becoming colder instead of warmer! The Odden feature is a tongue of ice which forms in the Greenland sea every winter and has a vital role to play in the circulation of water deep in the oceans of the world. This tongue of ice failed to form in the winters of 1993 and 1994 as the ice surrounding the North Pole slowly retreats. So little is known about the deep currents in the oceans that the effects of a change like this are incalculable but could be very far-reaching indeed.

Let us now move from global warming to that other pressing atmospheric problem – ozone depletion. We have already mentioned the problems associated with this so we need only recap here.

The ozone layer protects us from damaging UVB and UVC radiation. UVB has been the cause of many deaths from skin cancer already and deaths from this form of cancer are now second only to lung cancer in Europe. If the process of ozone depletion continues – if in fact the 'ozone hole' were to become worldwide – then skin cancer would rapidly overtake lung cancer and probably every other lethal disease as the number one killer. Our houses would have to be glazed with glass with zero UV transmission and we would have to be fully covered and wear effective sunglasses whenever we went outdoors. What a life! The oceanic plankton, which forms the base of the food webs, is very susceptible to excessive UV radiation and would probably be

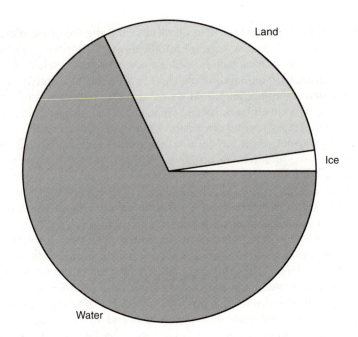

Figure 9.5   *Land, water and ice on the Earth's surface*

wiped out. This in turn would mean the end of fish, whales, and all other sea creatures. On land, our crops would also be devastated and it is hard to see how technology could produce sufficient food to supply the needs of the present world population, let alone that in the future.

The thought of unrestrained UV radiation raining down on the Earth brings us closest to the 'Gaia hypothesis'. Gaia was the Greek goddess of the Earth and the hypothesis is that the Earth is a system of living things and natural processes in balance which will react to throw out any disruptive influence. Up to this point the Gaia hypothesis looks very like the idea of the biosphere being made up of a series of balanced ecosystems which we have explored already. However, the Gaia hypothesis goes further, in suggesting that anything which disrupts this natural harmony will be eliminated so that the system can return to its harmonious balance. We don't have to look very far to see what the disruptive element is – US!

So, on the Gaia hypothesis, we will be eliminated and the planet will return to a balanced state without us. Truly a doomsday scenario for the human species but perhaps not for the planet as a whole. Undoubtedly, if we *were* eliminated and there were remaining life forms on the planet, they would slowly re-build the ozone layer, UV radiation would be reduced and evolution could start afresh. However, it seems more likely that we will continue as a disruptive element and the situation will gradually deteriorate until our ingenuity and instinct for self-preservation leads to a reversal of the decline.

Global warming and ozone depletion are, unfortunately, by no means the only problems we have to solve. Many of the other aspects of pollution that we have discussed in this book can be to varying degrees life-threatening. Agricultural chemicals and industrial wastes cause a whole range of disease, not least of all various cancers. Motor vehicle exhaust emissions not only contribute to acid rain, ozone depletion, and global warming, but can cause direct, and sometimes fatal, damage to our health.

We have already examined the effects of lead from exhausts but need to say a little more about ozone. Ozone, you may remember, is not produced directly by motor vehicle exhausts, but as a result of atmospheric oxygen combining with nitrogen oxides from exhaust fumes. These reactions are promoted by strong sunlight and the buildup of ozone is worst where traffic fumes become trapped as in large towns or towns surrounded by hills. In these conditions a photochemical 'smog' develops which impairs the respiratory functions of healthy individuals but can be fatal to those suffering from asthma, bronchitis, or other pulmonary afflictions. There is increasing evidence to link the incidence of asthma, especially in children, with the concentration of exhaust emissions.

Ozone in concentrations one-half to one-third that which are considered hazardous to humans can cause serious damage to many plants. Food crops such as tomatoes, beans, and oats can be severely damaged or even killed by such levels of ozone. It has been found that forest trees around Los Angeles have suffered an annual mortality rate of three per cent for the past 30 years which has now been directly linked to ozone derived from vehicle emissions. As a result of the damage from vehicle exhausts, it is no longer profitable to grow crops such as citrus fruits and tobacco around Los Angeles.

Ozone also damages many materials, particularly synthetic ones. Damage to car tyres from ozone in polluted areas is more significant than normal wear! Many building materials such as plastics and paints are broken down by ozone and this contributes significantly to maintenance costs in towns. So the doomsday scenario as far as vehicle generated ozone is concerned is that our crops fail, our buildings fall down, and it is just a question of whether we die of starvation or whether we are hit by a falling building before or after we die of lung failure!

Perhaps the ultimate doomsday prediction must come from the projections of population numbers.

You only have to think back to the exponential graphs we showed earlier to see that this situation simply cannot go on. The situation is made especially desperate by the fact that the greatest rates of population increase are to be found in the areas of greatest deprivation, food shortage, and pollution.

The history of the human species has many examples of people moving on when local conditions become intolerable. But what happens when there is nowhere to move to? One of the most abiding images of the 1980s and 1990s must surely be the terrible refugee camps in many parts of the world.

So far we have concentrated on the physical effects of a deterioration in our environment. But what about the effects of such deteriorating trends for the progress of society? Will overcrowding, shortage of food, disease, and a generally unpleasant environment lead to increasing unrest and a move towards chaos? Perhaps a term waiting to be invented is 'de-civilization'?

We may see this already happening in some African states where civil unrest is the norm and violence and starvation prevail. This situation is not so far from our own shores and one only has to look to the fringes of Europe to see a similar pattern emerging. Of course it couldn't happen in UK, could it? Well think again. Perhaps in a modified way it is creeping in. In a way this is an extension of the theme of personal success in which individuals in society are valued for their ability to achieve, sometimes at the expense of those around them.

It is naturally assumed that with personal achievement and success comes a sense of personal responsibility. But is that true? If you think about it, many of our 'successful' associates lead lives which are anything but responsible in environment terms. Often success is matched with a 'high energy' lifestyle. Fast cars, international jet travel ... a whole range of things that are unsustainable unless of course we accept that one person's access to these things is at the expense of others. Taking this a few stages further both in developing and developed societies, survival of a few at the expense of the majority is perhaps an unwelcome direction in which things are heading. On a national scale will it perhaps be that some countries will have small enough populations for them to lead privileged high energy lifestyles at the expense of developing countries?

Are developing countries going to go along with that? Already we have seen that some developing countries are refusing to take any responsibility for tackling environmental problems, which they blame on the developed nations. Their view is that, if areas such as Europe, North America, and Japan want to cut down emissions of carbon dioxide, for example, then they must pay for the setting up of clean power stations and industries in the developing countries at no additional cost to those countries.

Just like our 'yuppie' associate above, the developed countries want access to clean, unpolluted air and water, but want the developing countries to bear the cost. Is that really likely, or an acceptable position to take?

Perhaps an alternative trend is towards a more ordered society in which individual freedom is limited so that all have a greater share in what is available. Furthermore, with an ordered society some of the great problems of policy-making and the implementation of cohesive, widespread schemes for the good of all are made easier. This trend of course smacks of totalitarianism and of suppression of the independence of individuals. Furthermore, who has a realistic view of what may be done for the 'collective good'?

What we *can* do, however, is to look at some of the ways in which the problems we have examined could be tackled. The doomsday scenario is pretty scary and there are many different opinions as to how it may be avoided. What seems to be generally agreed, however, is that it *must* be avoided. We simply cannot go on as we are and must instead seek approaches that will lead us to a sustainable future.

THE HOPEFUL SCENARIO ... A SUSTAINABLE OPTION

There are heartening signs that we can make the adjustment towards a sustainable future, but first we need to examine the term 'sustainable'. It is perhaps a bit misleading. It implies that there is some adjustment or 'fix' we can apply to our *current* modes of living in order to sustain what we now have. This is unlikely to be the case. Sustainability is perhaps more a fundamental idea which embodies the measures we must take to ensure a long-term future for humanity itself. A definition of what is 'sustainable' is not easy to provide. It might mean adopting a lifestyle that can be continued for the foreseeable future without producing irreversible damage to the environment.

What, then, are the characteristics of a 'sustainable future'? The Brundtland Report, mentioned earlier, considered this question in great depth but the key idea emerging was that what was needed was *sustainable development*. This was defined as 'development that meets the needs of the present without compromising the ability of future generations to meet their own needs'.

There is a very important principle embodied in this approach which distinguishes *wants* from *needs*. As we have already seen with regard to the use of the motor car and the 'yuppie' lifestyle in general, the concept of emphasizing personal wants over needs – both one's own and the needs of others – is not really a sustainable environmental option.

A situation in which the wants of the developed countries of the world are pursued without taking any cognizance of the needs of the less developed countries can only lead to a situation in which environmental deterioration will get worse. As we have already seen, the less developed countries will not be willing to invest in measures to protect the global environment until they see the developed nations putting their own house in order and emphasizing the needs of all over their own, selfish, wants.

So how are we to get out of this bind we have got ourselves into? All nations want to develop, yet more development seems to lead inevitably to more environmental deterioration. Many ideas and options have been proposed but all can be roughly categorized into two groups: the 'Technological Fix' solutions and the 'Alternative Technology' solutions. We will examine the 'Technological Fix' approach first.

Technological Fix solutions

It cannot be denied that technology has, ever since the Industrial Revolution, provided us with great benefits. Poverty, disease and physical hardship have all been reduced whilst our opportunities for recreation, travel and cultural activities have all increased.

On the other hand, decline in the quality of the environment, social alienation, a widening gap between rich and poor, and depletion of resources represent the downside. While accepting that most of our current problems have been brought about by technology – especially industrial technology – the proponents of the Technological Fix would claim that this merely indicates that the technology which produced these problems was not sufficiently developed. Through the development of better technologies all these problems can be solved.

We can examine this approach by reference to three major areas of concern: pollution, depletion of resources, and population increase.

Pollution

Pollution first. The basic reason why industry produces pollutants is that there is no compulsion on the polluter to avoid this. Unless the 'polluter pays' principle becomes mandatory worldwide, the economic advantages are all in favour of not avoiding pollution. It is simply much cheaper to discharge industrial waste into a convenient local river than to have it re-processed to a non-polluting form.

The Technological Fix argument is that, as industry advances and becomes more profitable, the cost differential between dumping and re-processing waste narrows relative to profits and so, eventually, the benefits of gaining a better image for the industry outweigh the extra costs. It is also said that the consumer must be expected to bear some of the 'clean-up' costs and that, as these issues become better understood, this additional cost will become more acceptable.

There are plenty of examples to show that technology can avoid pollution in this way. For example, the installation of 'scrubbers' and electrostatic depositors in power station chimneys can remove some gaseous and particulate pollutants – but at a cost. Similarly, nitrate pollution of drinking water can be removed by the installation of expensive deionizing plant. If we, the consumers, are prepared to pay the extra cost then we can have a higher quality of drinking water on tap.

Yes, technology is capable of removing most, if not all, the pollution which we currently face. But are the shareholders prepared to accept the lower dividends or the directors reductions in their huge salaries and the consumers increases in the price they pay for goods and services in order to achieve this?

Resource depletion

The second area of concern we identified above was depletion of resources, both of materials and of usable energy. Given that industry by definition uses resources, can the Technological Fix offer any solutions here? How about supplies of materials such as iron, copper, aluminium, coal, or oil? These are finite resources which must eventually run out.

Well, the Fixers have three answers.

Firstly, technological advances allow us to extract materials from lower and lower grades of the crude supply source. For example, aluminium is now routinely extracted economically from sources which, in the 1930s, were considered quite useless. In fact, in many cases these advances in extraction methods have resulted in the accessible reserves actually *increasing* faster than the rate at which reserves are being used up. Of course, even these reserves will eventually run out but, say the Fixers, that time is being pushed so far into the future that, before it comes, we will have found alternatives.

This, then, is the second solution: the development of alternative materials to replace those which may eventually run out. Synthetic materials have already replaced metals in many applications, and there have been some spectacular successes, such as carbon fibre. A carbon fibre bicycle is lighter, stronger – and faster – than its metal equivalent. It is expensive, but with increased volume of production the costs will come down.

There is, however, one question which must be asked. Where do these synthetic materials come from? Unfortunately, in many cases, the answer is that they are derived from oil! Nevertheless, many useful synthetic materials are derived from non-oil bases and so this option cannot be discounted. Note, however, that producing these materials usually requires a great deal more energy than producing the materials they are designed to replace!

So this brings us to the third option – recycling. Here we are a bit closer to the 'alternative technology' camp. Today, some cars are being advertised as 'completely recyclable'. The manufacturers obviously see this as a good selling point, although they don't mention the cost of recycling your BMW! But there is a good point here. Not many years ago, when something broke on your car, the first place to seek a replacement was not the shiny, expensive spares department of the Main Agent, it was the breaker's yard! So recycling of car parts is not a new idea but it does have cost implications, especially as it is necessarily labour-intensive. Our experience with cars highlights the major difficulty with most recycling efforts.

Few products are made of one material. Even if you remove the metal caps from glass bottles they often have that annoying little ring of metal left around the neck! Paper and card are relatively easy to recycle, but separating the paper from the printing ink is well nigh impossible, so the product is grey instead of white. Of course it can be bleached, but that introduces another pollutant! Aluminium cans seem a good bet – so long as they are all aluminium! Some cans have a coated steel body with an aluminium top and bottom. And then, of course, there are those with a plastic 'widget' inside! Cars, of course, are a complete mix of steel, plastic, copper, rubber, aluminium, glass, paint, and fabric, so separating out that lot is not easy!

Techniques to separate out these mixtures of materials *have* improved dramatically in recent years but, again, the cost of this often makes the product more expensive than using raw materials, and the processes are usually energy intensive. The greatest challenge to the Technological Fix must surely be the problem of non-renewable energy resources.

Sources of energy

Fossil fuels have been the rootstock of rapid industrialization in the developed world. For the Technological Fixers the primary concern about fossil fuels is their finite nature and what we will do when they run out.

Environmental concern has to an extent replaced fears of energy starvation. Leaving fossil fuels in the ground as a fossilized testament to the rise of the plant kingdom is an increasingly attractive proposition!

As we have seen, there are some disadvantages to the way we currently gain our supplies of energy. Fossil fuels have been cheap, versatile, and abundant but we are now aware that they are having a significant effect on our surroundings. In this respect they possess all the qualities of an economic drug. We are hooked on their undoubted benefits and are reluctant to face up to the challenge of rehabilitation. Surely there are other ways in which we can gain our energy supplies without being tied to the drug barons of the Carbon Club?

Yes of course there are, but choices will have to be made.

Oil, as we have seen, may run out in 40 years. There is plenty of coal in the Earth, but a lot of it is pretty difficult, and expensive, to get at. As a result, both Technological Fixers and Alternative Technologists are looking towards the greater use of so-called 'renewable' energy resources. The main sources, as far as the Fixers are concerned, are solar, wind, wave, and water power.

Where the Fixers differ from the Alternatives is that the Fixers claim we can go on expanding our use of energy because of the expansion of nuclear power and because technological advances will enable us to progressively replace current sources with these renewable sources. By contrast, the Alternatives, whilst considering other, less polluting forms of energy supply, are also much more concerned about ways of reducing energy demand. Undoubtedly there have been great advances in the power output of both solar powered and wind powered generating systems, but they are still a very long way from offering any substantial alternatives to the use of fossil fuels.

The other plank of the Fixers' solution, the nuclear option, is perhaps the most obvious, yet the most controversial.

The nuclear option

There is no doubt that supplies of nuclear fuel on the Earth are virtually inexhaustible. Modern nuclear plants are far more efficient than their predecessors and, if suitably expanded, could certainly replace all existing electricity generating systems. With the development of advanced electrically powered vehicles there seems no reason why the burning of precious fossil fuels should not stop completely thus releasing them for the production of far more valuable synthetic materials. There are no problems with gaseous emissions and nuclear waste is minimal, if highly toxic and for varying lengths of time.

Do we hear shouts of 'What about Chernobyl?' and 'Have you forgotten Windscale and Three Mile Island?' Three nuclear superpowers having a nuclear accident each is a powerful reminder that poor management of the nuclear beast may lead to terrible retribution.

Certainly, safety is an issue, but these accidents related to old-fashioned, out-of-date plants. Modern plants, we are assured, have such extensive fail-safe mechanisms built into them that human error – the basic cause of these accidents – can be totally eliminated. The plants will be totally under the control of 100 per cent reliable machines. The computers running these plants are far more reliable than humans and they simply do not make mistakes.

Well ... maybe? You've never known a computer to make an error, have you?

Let's assume the Fixers are right and that future nuclear plants will never go wrong. What about all that nuclear waste? As we saw earlier, this stuff is going to be with us for thousands of years. There is no Technological Fix either now or in the foreseeable future which will make it possible to safely dispose of nuclear waste. If the projected increase in the numbers of nuclear plants worldwide was to take place then the amount of nuclear waste accumulating would become a massive problem and perhaps the most serious environmental hazard of all time.

This, then, is the great stumbling block. Unless the nuclear waste problem can be solved then the option of replacing all current fossil fuel based generating plants with nuclear ones is simply not a sustainable option at all.

Yet the nuclear industry is set to grow. In the UK about 25 per cent of the electricity is generated from nuclear stations. Just over the Channel in France the figure is a staggering 70 per cent. The cost of electricity from nuclear powered installations is low, just as long as one writes off the cost of decommissioning and decontaminating old stations. Even this cost will fall as specialist companies gain experience of this complex process.

Well into the twenty-first century it may be that nuclear fusion rather than fission becomes the way ahead for the nuclear industry. It would certainly be a magnificent achievement. The idea of combining (fusing) matter to release energy as in our own Sun is very attractive. Fusion power stations would be like little bottled Suns beaming out intense energy and with fewer problems of nuclear waste. The fuel source for such nuclear plants would be hydrogen in its various isotope forms. This is readily available in virtually unlimited quantities from water in the seas. The by-products are helium, a harmless and useful gas, and neutrons which are not so friendly.

And what of the so-called renewables, surely they are part of the way ahead? Certainly from the viewpoint of the diversification of sources of energy supply they are well worth developing, but they are by no means a technological alternative as mass energy producers.

'Renewable' energy sources

Let us examine a few of the options which are currently open to us. These energy sources (excluding tidal and geothermal) are derived more or less directly from the Sun.

A growing number of sites in the UK have wind 'farms' and they make a very small contribution to our energy requirements, as long as it is windy that is. Of course, most sites are on exposed hillsides where sustained high windspeeds are encountered and this is where the trouble starts. Many claim that these structures are an intrusion into natural landscapes. The soft swishing of giant blades is another aspect of noise pollution which is unwanted by those who live or walk near wind farms. Public concern could certainly limit their spread on the UK mainland. It is possible that banks of offshore wind turbines could become a partial solution. Interestingly in Denmark, a land without a rich fossil fuel heritage, wind turbines are visible from virtually any perspective on the rural landscape and appear to be an accepted part of a culture of energy efficiency. Currently, the UK government offers a subsidy to producers of electricity from wind farms. In this way the pace of wind energy research and development can continue and thus each generation of wind farms becomes more effective in the energy transfer process.

What about biomass? Simply burning raw or processed growth material from plant matter which is constantly re-planted does not add to carbon dioxide emissions. This gas is recycled in the ongoing sequence of carbon dioxide intake, growth, harvesting, burning, and further gaseous release. Energy from biomass can be realized from a number of sources. It can be achieved by gaining alcohol-related products from sugar cane or potatoes. It can even be achieved by simply burning straw. It can be obtained from crushing the oil from a variety of crops and by burning coppiced willow.

A key question is to what extent we can allow ourselves the luxury of growing energy rather than growing food? Energy farming takes up a great deal of space. Even then the economics of transporting high bulk, low value fuels has to be taken into account.

Nevertheless, biomass is a viable source. It does diversify our energy portfolio and there are for example a growing number of specialized power stations to deal with various biomass products. An increasing number of cars, lorries and buses will use alcohol and oilseed products. In the longer term, it is possible that we will only allow ourselves the luxury of versatile, harvested oils for use as lubricants and as energy intensive fuels in the aviation industry. A growing number of power stations in northern Europe will look to willow coppices and huge bales of straw as a by-product from cereal growing for their fuel rather than coal, gas, and oil.

Hydro-electric projects have a well established role in electricity generation and will continue to be developed. However, it may be that large projects in environmentally valued settings which flood vast areas of land and produce electricity for certain industrial processes will no longer catch the public imagination. We will examine the problems created by one such development shortly.

We will follow up these ideas further as we examine the Alternative Technology option but first we will examine what is, perhaps, the greatest challenge to the Technological Fix approach.

Population expansion

The Technological Fix answer to population is really quite simple – birth control devices. In the 1960s the use of the contraceptive pill became widespread and was seen then as the great technological breakthrough which would finally solve the population problem. Undoubtedly this did have a major effect in developed countries where, in many cases, it sparked off something not far short of a social revolution. In less developed countries there were greater difficulties. Even when large sums of money were made available to supply the pill, mainly through United Nations agencies, success depended upon the women taking the pill every day without fail. This burden of individual responsibility was something to which the Technological Fix had no solution. The only way to make this work was through social and educational means.

A further blow to the pill as the great salvation of the world was felt when doubts were raised about safety and side effects. Of course, technology did succeed in solving these medical problems to a large extent, but the Technological Fix had no answer to the personal and social problems.

The next great breakthrough was seen in the 1970s with the widespread introduction of the intra-uterine contraceptive device, or IUD. This was heralded by the Technological Fixers as being the greatest contribution of the century to population control. It was claimed that this would finally provide the solution to the problems of 'excessive' numbers and also of personal motivation and social pressure. It was widely accepted that relying on men to operate birth control measures was unsuccessful and the pill had shown that this was also a problem for women. Now the IUD would take the responsibility away from the individuals once fitted. Of course there was still the cost of supply and fitting, but with United Nations help this was tackled and there is no doubt that it did make a considerable contribution at the time, but the problem is still far from solved.

What the Technological Fix cannot deal with is social values in which men consider the number of children they father as a measure of their virility and where contraception is opposed on religious grounds.

The other way in which the Technological Fix approach sees a solution to the population problem is far more indirect and long-term. We have already seen how technological advances can contribute to the improvement in food supplies but this is only the start. It is claimed that the development of a more effective industrial base coupled with improvement in food supplies will eventually reduce starvation and poverty to a point where birth rates will begin to decline, as they have in the developed countries.

Let us look back, in Figure 8.4, at the population pyramid patterns for developed and less developed countries we saw earlier.

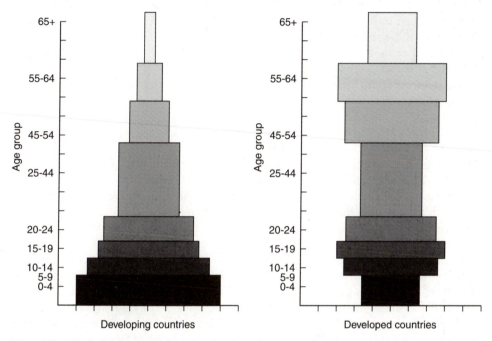

Figure 9.6 *Population pyramids of developed and developing countries*

The idea is that, with growing wealth, the less developed countries will move from the pattern on the left, with high birth rates giving a larger proportion of children and young people, to the pattern on the right showing a lowered birth rate and lowered death rate. In South America and some parts of Asia, although the total population increase is still a problem, there is evidence that there has been a shift to this lower birth/lower death rate pattern. The argument implies that what is needed is not so much birth control as economic development and increased food production. Naturally, this solution is the option preferred by those religions opposed to contraception.

The question which still remains to be answered is how to bring this economic development about. The very countries that need help to develop are the ones which are burdened by huge loan and interest repayments to the financiers of the developed nations. Unless the developed nations are prepared to forgo some of their options for further development, or indeed some of their prosperity, it is hard to see how this 'economic miracle' in the less developed nations is to be brought about.

Alternative Technology solutions

Now let us turn to the other scenario, that of alternative technology.

In the developed countries of the world, how much of the working day is spent earning money or sitting in a car? What is the purpose of all this work? For many people the answer to this question is that they are primarily engaged in mass-producing, directly or indirectly, increasingly sophisticated products which others are persuaded to buy whether they really need them or not. Of course, we as teachers cannot be accused of falling into this category!

The Alternative Technology philosophy is fundamentally concerned with lifestyle, although it can be most easily recognized by the forms of technology employed. It emphasizes the small-scale production of the things society needs through social patterns and economic institutions which are very different from the Western-style, high energy pattern.

This is an important idea to which we will return, but let us first examine some of the low-tech alternatives to the industrial processes which have caused many of our present problems.

We will start with the important question of energy resources, which we have already alluded to in relation to the Technological Fix.

The high-tech approach to using solar energy is to design sophisticated solar collectors either to heat water directly or to direct the radiant energy onto solar cells which transfer this to electrical energy. The low-tech Alternative Technology approach will often use the principle of having a large, blackened 'collector plate' to collect the solar energy and transfer this to heat. The heat is then carried away by water either trickling over the surface of the collector or by pipes embedded behind the collector plate through which water is circulated. This is only really efficient in countries with sufficient sunlight and these are countries where hot water is perhaps not so important. However, in countries such as Cyprus, all the domestic hot water for a house can be provided for much of the year by this method with a consequent saving of non-renewable energy supplies. In many less-developed countries a more important use of solar energy is for cooking. The principle is to build a curved reflector which will bring the sun's rays to focus at a point in front of the reflector. Food placed at this point can then be cooked very effectively (see the diagram in Figure 9.7).

Using solar power is not new, but improvements in design have been brought about by research in various countries, and this information can help developing countries make better use of this technology.

Wind power is probably one of the oldest 'alternative' power sources and can be used to drive anything that requires rotation, from grinding mills to water pumps to electricity generators. Because wind is a more readily available power source in most developed countries than sun, quite large sums of research money have been put into improving wind turbine design in these countries. Again, this technology could be provided freely to developing countries who cannot afford to do the research themselves but could make good use of the know-how.

Water power has probably been used by humans as long as wind power and, once again, modern turbine designs are much more efficient than old style water wheels. The provision of small hydroelectric power plants which can be used in quite small river flows could be invaluable to many developing countries yet the developed countries seem more interested in funding vast and environmentally damaging dam projects, which have far less impact on the wellbeing of the majority of people than could be achieved through the provision of larger numbers of small plants.

A classic example of this situation has arisen in India where the Narmada River scheme will probably be the largest scheme based on large-scale dam technology

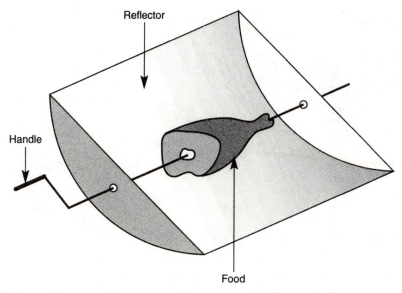

Figure 9.7 *A solar cooker*

anywhere in the world and is expected to take 50 years to complete. The funding for this vast project has come from the developed countries, by way of the World Bank, and will involve the building of 30 major dams, 135 smaller ones with around 3,000 minor dams. Although this scheme, when completed, will produce a great deal of electricity and will provide irrigation for 20,000 square kilometres of land in areas which currently suffer badly from droughts, it will also cause untold environmental damage. The project has attracted widespread opposition and protest since it will displace almost a quarter of a million people and will flood around 5,000 square kilometres of forest and fertile farmland. The opponents of this scheme point out that this project will only benefit the large, rich landowners whereas many smaller irrigation and local power generation schemes would have benefited all the people much more and at far lower cost.

Finally, we will look at biogas generation. In the developed countries the generation of methane in rubbish tips and from sewage plants is often considered a nuisance and the gas is just burnt off. Occasionally, the gas may be collected and used, as in some sewage plants.

By contrast, in China, Africa and India in particular, the development of biogas plants can make a valuable contribution to local fuel needs. The basic principle of a biogas plant is very simple. Organic material, such as a mixture of cow dung and shredded stalks of a plant crop, are mixed with water in a container which could be anything from a concrete container to an old oil drum. The organic matter decomposes and, as it does so, it releases methane gas which can then be piped to cooking stoves or into a generator which produces electricity. In many villages in China two-thirds of the electricity supply comes from such biogas plants. The gas produced is the same as is released directly by the cow's gut, but it is easier to collect it from a biogas chamber than to plug a lot of cows into the supply pipes! Figure 9.8 illustrates biogas production.

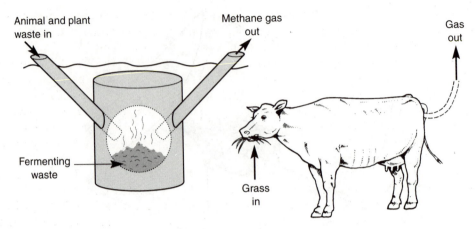

Figure 9.8   *Engineered and natural biogas production*

No-one is suggesting that these alternative technology solutions could be applied directly to the developed countries to replace existing high-tech methods. What is certain is that there would be better value for money and less environmental damage would be caused if the development of such technologies in the less developed countries were to be assisted by the developed nations instead of them putting huge sums in potential 'white elephants' such as the Narmada River scheme.

So far, we have looked at sustainability from a world perspective, but what about closer to home? Are there things we can do to improve the situation in the developed nations of the world? Are we so closely tied to the high-tech approach that we are stuck with it?

Perhaps not, but we need to look carefully at what we do now and what lessons we might learn from some of the alternative technologies being developed in the less-developed nations of the world. This is one of the lessons we have to learn. The assumption that the less-developed nations can only learn from us, and not the other way round, is not only arrogant, it cuts us off from a whole lot of valuable learning and experience.

We have seen how a number of alternative energy sources might be made available, but we are stuck for the foreseeable future with the ones we have got. So how can we limit the damage and give ourselves more time to develop alternatives? One key aspect of a sustainable future will be concerned with energy efficiency. Corresponding in some ways to this at a personal level is 'low energy living'. Instead of getting bogged down in definitions let us look at the example of energy efficiency to try to get a clearer picture of just what a sustainable future might involve for us all.

Energy efficiency

There is of course an element of technological fix in all of this. Energy efficiency is one aspect of a move towards sustainability that can be made on a large or small scale. Let's start at the beginning – where the energy supply comes from.

Power stations are a good starting point. In the mid-1990s our fossil-fuelled power stations waste on average 65 per cent of the fuel they burn. This means that they are 35 per cent efficient. Unusable low-grade heat is lost to the environment.

This less than 100 per cent efficiency is inevitable as it reflects one of the laws of thermodynamics that states that you cannot transfer all of the energy available as heat from burning, say, coal or oil into the kinetic energy of a spinning shaft to turn a generator. However these power stations are not working at *maximum* efficiency. There is also an economic perspective that to make our stock of conventional coal-fired power stations more efficient would cost a great deal of development money. Is it worth it?

In the UK there has been a massive shift away from conventional coal-fuelled power stations to combined cycle gas turbines. In these stations an extra stage of heat recovery makes the generating process less wasteful. Combined cycle gas turbine electricity generating stations are about 58 per cent efficient, but they are based on relatively small reserves of natural gas rather than the couple of hundred years reserves of coal. On the face of it, the switch to gas has many advantages, but many of these have a short-term perspective.

Combined cycle power stations are rapidly built, flexibly controlled by very few staff and, on raw costing, produce very cheap electricity. Compared to coal- or oil-fired stations, on the basis of similar electrical output they emit smaller quantities of potentially harmful gases. This includes sulphur dioxide which has done so much to damage the lakes and forests of Scandinavia through acid rain. The Swedes in particular are delighted with the switch to gas! Within the scope of conventional electricity generation by power stations, gas is efficient as a fuel.

However, as you will see shortly, this viewpoint is comparative. In overall energy terms, gas burnt to produce electricity at power stations is less efficient in the overall energy transfer process than taking gas supplies to our homes and letting us use it for cooking and heating.

You've got the electricity in your home, but how efficiently are you going to use it?

The energy efficiency of central heating systems is an area in which significant gains have been made in recent years. For example, new gas condensing boilers are around 85 per cent efficient in extracting the heat from burning gas and transferring it to hot water. Standard gas-fired boilers are only around 70 per cent efficient. You will note that this simple domestic energy transfer is still significantly more efficient than that achieved in combined cycle power stations. But of course power stations produce the ever-flexible electricity, whereas at home we can only heat up water and food with gas.

Even the humble refrigerator can be made more energy efficient. Some new varieties of fridge are up to three times more efficient than devices of similar capacity produced 20 years ago. But like the gas condensing boilers they cost more than their standard counterparts. Is the extra worth it? This is really a problem for more than just the accountant who, as we are often reminded, knows the cost of everything and the value of nothing!

In schools, children can identify the energy ratings for a range of electrical devices. Tape recorders, computers and light bulbs are rated in watts to show the electrical energy which is converted during their use.

The concept of **power** is available from discussions about electrical devices, for it is a combination of measurements. We must look at both the energy rating and the time the device operates to give us an indication of power. Power is **rate** of energy conversion. A one kilowatt (that is a thousand watts) electric fire glowing for one hour would have a power rating of one kilowatt hour, or a **unit** of electricity. You will recognize this from your electricity bill.

By collecting data from home children can look at the watts rating for example on electric hovering lawn mowers and electric cylinder mowers. The cylinder types are around four times more energy efficient since they do not require large electric motors to drive fans to hold them on a cushion of air as well as cut the grass!

Electric light bulbs are another source for investigation. Typical incandescent light bulbs are rated at between 60 and 100 watts. Fluorescent bulbs of similar light output are rated at only 18 to 25 watts. They are around four times more energy efficient. How can this be? The answer can be found if you have ever come uncomfortably close to a standard light bulb. They are hot. A standard light bulb is more of a 'heat bulb' than a light bulb! About 80 per cent of the electrical energy is transferred to heat, not to light.

Children can count the numbers of light bulbs in use in their homes. They can see how many are of the energy efficient fluorescent type. Happily, although energy efficient light bulbs (and tubes of course) are expensive, the pay-back period is relatively short if they are used in places which are lit up for long periods, such as principal rooms, hall, stairs, and landings. In some instances, the pay-back is within one year.

In schools we already encourage energy consciousness and efficiency through shutting doors and windows in winter and turning off lights when they are not needed. These messages need to be carried back into homes along with a sound rationale for energy efficiency that can only be developed via discussions with teachers.

Why do we shut the doors and windows – to keep the heat in of course! But what about all that heat that gets out through the *closed* doors and windows? Consider also the walls, roof and floor?

So another aspect of energy efficiency is insulation. The building regulations in the UK have progressively specified more stringent standards for walls, roofs and floors. The 'U' value which is used to express insulation is a measure based on thermal transfer. A 'U' value of say 0.45 means that 0.45 watts of energy is transferred through one square metre of structure for each degree Celsius of temperature contrast, i.e. the difference in temperature between the internal and the external surfaces of the structure.

Putting it another way, consider just a square metre of external house wall. If the temperature inside is to be maintained at 20 degrees Celsius and the temperature outside the building is 0 degrees the contrast is 20 degrees. 0.45 watts multiplied by each degree Celsius is nine watts. This means that nine watts of energy will be transferred through this square metre of wall in this particular temperature contrast regime. For an external wall with an area of ten square metres the transfer would be 90 watts. For a small detached house with 400 square metres of external walls (forget the windows for simplicity) the heat 'loss' – or transfer – with this 20 degrees Celsius temperature contrast would be 3.6 kilowatts. If this goes on for one hour it will cost you just over three and a half units of electricity.

Modern houses are now constructed to thermal insulation standards nearly three times higher than they were 20 years ago. Their heating bills are therefore three times lower. Clearly for new-build situations there is great economic sense in putting in significant quantities of insulation. For older properties, especially those with solid brick walls which cannot be cavity insulated the future is rather bleak. Retro-fitting of external insulation panels is extremely expensive and, in present economic terms, not seen as cost-effective.

So what will persuade us to consider energy efficiency in our lives? Will it be that we will purchase expensive energy efficient devices because we realize for example that we are reducing gaseous emissions and thus having less impact on greenhouse gases and global climatic change?

The chain of actions and consequences is long and tenuous. It is also possible to say 'why me'? *Someone else* should use their car less often or install an energy efficient central heating boiler.

A shift in thinking may be linked to politics. A change in the way that taxation is levied may be just one way in which changes can occur. Simply, taxation on fuel and power will heighten consciousness of the need to reduce consumption, and indeed enable us to look at our ranking of energy priorities in the way that we live our lives. 'Let the polluter pay' means you the user of energy! But this is very much a political hot potato which few policy designers wish to grasp.

So, taxes are increased on fuel and power. Good for energy consciousness and the environment. But let us take a specific example within this concept. If a political party wished to undermine this policy it could simply pick up on the quite valid point that this extra taxation load would affect, say, air travel. As a consequence headlines in the daily newspapers would read 'Now they are going to tax our holidays! Is nothing sacred!' Perhaps with imagination, vision, and a great deal of public consultation, the whole basis of our tax system could be revised so that we are taxed according to how we live our lives in relation to environmental impact. Those with high energy lifestyles will pay more. Those with least environmental impact will pay less. Such a basis for taxation would replace current taxes with indirect taxation on fuel and power. If, of course, taxes on fuel and power are simply added to the overall burden of taxation then no doubt the population will rebel. Additional taxes are never popular!

Current estimates suggest that as much as ten per cent of the current energy requirement of the UK can be met from renewable sources. But what of the other 90 per cent? Where will it come from in the future?

Perhaps we need to probe and challenge the thinking that maintains that we need a vast amount of energy – and that the forecasts for energy demand are set to continually climb. Is there another way ahead?

Low energy living

A sustainable future may well rest as much with low energy living as the use of energy efficient devices and the utilization of power sources which do not rely on fossil fuels. We need to explain at this point that our understanding of 'low energy living' goes beyond mere energy efficiency and energy source diversification. It is about attitudes to ourselves, our descendants, and all living things that share our planet. That is a pretty tall order! Where do we begin?

Lifestyle is a good place to start. There is a consistent and direct relationship in the developed world between high energy lifestyles and pollution. Let us interpret that through an everyday experience like going to the shops.

Life is really rather complicated. It is necessary sometimes to simplify ideas in order to get at the fundamental underlying principles involved. Let us look at a grossly oversimplified example which nevertheless makes the point.

The smart way to shop?

On closing the front door we get into that chic little car beloved of the advertisements and drive out on the by-pass to the new out-of-town shopping centre. There is easy parking and the environment seems secure and inviting. We put the car alarm on anyway. Overhead, a tower with a TV surveillance camera keeps an ever-watchful eye on things.

But wait a moment. What is the true cost of all this convenience? Who or what is affected by our actions? Let us think it through – or at least try to!

Using the car as a one-person carrier is of course desperately fuel inefficient. The quick hop around the by-pass is deceptive. New roads destroy our surroundings in a number of subtle ways, they are not just a loss of landscape to concrete. They are built to take the strain off congested roads and speed traffic to and from where it needs to go. But although each new road has local impact and may be hailed as an environment saver, the overall effect is insidiously destructive. Each new road makes journeys by car that bit easier. We can weave ever more complex lifestyles around the convenience of fast roads and decentralized facilities and use our cars even more. More car use induces more pollution, more congestion, and the need for more roads. Think about it.

Sadly even the technological fix of the catalytic converter to exhaust systems is not as attractive as we would like to believe. It only works when the exhaust system is hot, say after travelling a couple of miles. And the majority of car journeys are short ones!

The out-of-town shopping centre and car park were built on low-cost farmland. At night time it is dead and locked up. At the same time the city centre is in decline. Many shops are closed and vagrants roam the streets. They cannot get out as far as the out-of-town shopping centre and anyway they would be kicked out when the shops shut down. There is talk of crime on the streets. It is difficult to park in the town centre and the buses there are just plain inconvenient, not to mention the stench of diesel fumes. Ugh!

A smarter way to shop?

There is another way. The low energy lifestyle way. It reflects attitudes to planning and political will as much as it does to technological fixes. It also reflects a degree of social care and consideration which is based more widely upon understanding actions and consequences.

You leave the house and breathe cleaner air. Fewer diesel particulates are floating about and that ozone-induced smog seems to have cleared away. You walk the short distance (ah, exercise) to a sheltered waiting point. Soon your conveyance arrives. Almost silently an electrically powered tram glides along the centre of the road. The fare is cheap. A switch of funding from roads to urban light rail has occurred.

Reduced emissions have reduced the number of children with asthma, and therefore reduced costs to the hospital budget have released funds for assisting the former vagrants. The streets are full of people walking. There is less crime. Direct car crime, car-related crime and injuries have declined because there are fewer cars that people want to use. The horrors of joyriding and car-borne escapes from scenes of crime begin to fade from our memory. Funds formerly spent on the road traffic division of the police force, hospital casualty department, and judicial services have been diverted to city centre enhancement programmes. Car parks have now become just parks. Former fume-ridden noisy pavements have been widened to accommodate street cafes. The city centre is alive at night. Personal mobility is not compromised – just the means by which this is achieved.

Is this all pie in the sky? There are signs of visionary thinking. Let us take an example from Richard Rogers' series of Reith lectures, published in the *Independent*, Monday 20 February 1995. Rogers, one of the leading architects of our time, shares his view of the sense of social responsibility and consultation with the public which needs to be taken into account in the planning of cities if they are to become sustainable. He proposes a view of living in 'Compact City' and the changes that have to be made to our attitudes to cars:

> Just the anticipation of high levels of car use had made city planners design new cities around road specifications. The tail is wagging the dog . . .
>
> The new form of dense and diverse city is the Compact City. The first benefit of the compact approach is that the countryside is protected from the encroachment of urban development. For the citizen living in the city the compactness is relieved by a network of public spaces and parks. The Compact City would grow around centres of social and commercial activity. London's historic structure of towns, villages and parks is typical of this polycentric pattern of development – a social structure which focuses communities around neighbourhoods.
>
> These neighbourhoods would include a diversity of private activities and bring public services, including education and public transport as well as local work opportunities within convenient reach of the community. This proximity would reduce the need for driving for everyday needs, and make trams, light rail, electric buses, cycling and walking more pleasant and more effective. It would also increase conviviality and restore the natural policing of streets by an increased presence of people and deceased congestion and pollution from cars . . . Sustainable cities of this sort could, I contend, reassert the city as the social embodiment of a community-based society.'

As with taxation policy, a sense of vision coupled with imagination and determination is required. Public information, debate and decision-making is crucial.

This clearly is a matter of choice, based on advantages and disadvantages to personal lifestyles. But also it is a matter which involves consideration of actions and consequences. We can only make bold and imaginative decisions about our future if we are well-informed, open-minded, unselfish, and able to apply sound reasoning and judgement to a great wealth of freely available environmental data. Moreover, we need to communicate our findings to those who speak on our behalf.

This sounds like a political rallying call. It is not intended to be so, but if we are becoming uncomfortable with the way we are living our lives then we need to speak out.

CHILDREN ARE THE FUTURE

We hope of course that some attitudes such as being open-minded, and social attributes such as being unselfish, will be instilled in our school children.

The flow of information and promotion of discussion that leads to critical thinking and decision-making is in our hands as teachers. Discussions about choices related to actions and consequences are fundamental. Are you going to play your part?

In a way we have found the writing of this book has taken us through a whole range of emotions. Distress, concern and a need to communicate have all played their part. In many ways, it is communication which is the key and within that the ability to lead and inform constructive debate from reliable sources. We hope this book will have provided you with one such reliable source of information. We may all now share some of the concerns for the well-being of our planet and you are in an ideal position to influence what happens next. You, after all, are a primary teacher!

We leave you with some of the ideas in an American publication entitled *Getting Started: A Guide to Bringing Environmental Education Into Your Classroom* (ed. D. Bones, University of Michigan, 1994). In response to the question, what is environmental education?, we found this quote to be very helpful:

> Environmental education is more than teaching about the environment. It is about people. Environmental education stresses the exploration of attitudes and values, and the development of knowledge and skills, so that people can take an active part in decision-making in the world around them.

Five process areas in this publication are identified, they include:

Awareness.   This is gained both as sensory awareness of the world around us – think of all those firsthand skills in science – and an awareness of societal issues and problem-solving strategies. Teacher-led discussion and consideration of the viewpoints of others can help here. Within this, for example, environmental education is helping students become aware that there are choices they can make as consumers, and that there are many implications to the choices they make.

Knowledge.   This gives us an increased awareness which enables us to understand natural processes and to see these as a holistic entity, recognizing the interconnectedness of the world.

Attitudes.   We may certainly change and mature as we develop a deeper appreciation and respect for the natural world and for individual people and cultures.

Skills.   This is an important area in which we become more versatile in the gaining and interpretation of information. In essence, the development of process skills involves teaching students how to think, not what to think.

Lastly, there is *Participation.*   This is the key element that embodies awareness, knowledge, attitudes and skills.

If we are to apply these things plus our commitment beyond the classroom, then this involves us all. It means changing personal behaviour and involving ourselves in decisions affecting the school and further afield. Communicating your feelings to your MP is as much an expression of this as clearing a local pond of debris or planting wild flowers around the margins of the school playing fields.

It is up to us all.

Index